MAYDAY! MAYDAY!

**Curb immigration. Stop multiculturalism.
Or it's the end of the Canada we know!**

By Lowell Green

Spruce Ridge Publishing

ISBN 978-0-9813149-1-4
Printed and bound in Canada

This book was written, published, edited and printed in Canada without the aid of government grants of any nature.

Library and Archives Canada Cataloguing in Publication

Green, Lowell, 1936-

Mayday, Mayday : curb immigration and stop multiculturalism, or it's the end of the Canada we know / Lowell Green.

Includes bibliographical references.
ISBN 978-0-9813149-1-4

1. Canada—Emigration and immigration—Social aspects.
2. Multiculturalism—Canada. 3. Immigrants—Canada.
4. Refugees—Canada. I. Title.

JV7225.2.G74 2010 325.71 C2010-906017-2

This book is dedicated to our
immigrant ancestors whose blood, sweat, tears,
bravery, perseverance and love forged for us
this, the grandest country in the world, Canada!

Immigrant Eyes

Guy Clark, American singer and songwriter

Oh Ellis Island was swarming
Like a scene from a costume ball
Decked out in the colours of Europe
And on fire with the hope of it all
There my father's own father stood huddled
With the tired and hungry and scared
Turn of the century pilgrims
Bound by the dream that they shared
They were standing in lines just like cattle
Poked and prodded and shoved
Some were one desk away from sweet freedom
Some were torn from someone they love
Through this sprawling tower of Babel
Came a young man confused and alone
Determined and bound for America
And carryin' everything he owned.

Chorus
Sometimes when I look in my grandfather's immigrant eyes
I see that day reflected and I can't hold my feelings inside
I see—starting with nothing and working hard all of his life
Don't take this country for granted say
my grandfather's immigrant eyes

Now he rocks and stares out the window
But his eyes are still just as clear
As the day he sailed through the harbour
And came ashore on the island of tears
My grandfather's days are numbered
But I won't let his memory die
'Cause he gave me the gift of this country
And the look in his immigrant eyes.

(Reprinted with permission)

Contents

Foreword

This book will surely offend some. Finding offence is, after all, a national sport in Canada these days. Human Rights Commissions have been established to ensure proper punishment. I offer as my only defense the following thoughts in support of this book from one of the Capital's most distinguished and accomplished men:

Multiculturalism, Political Correctness, and Freedom of Speech

By Andy Haydon, former Regional Chair of Ottawa-Carleton

The pernicious doctrine of multiculturalism, which teaches free people to belittle their own national culture, while bending their knees to tyrants, results in the removal of Western freedoms—above all the foundational and fundamental freedom—freedom of speech!

Multiculturalism is a peculiar set of attitudes that exalts individual minority groups of foreign cultures and treats their values as sacrosanct and equal in every way to the values that our forebearers and we have fought so hard to obtain and retain in this country.

The freedom we enjoy in the West is a precious, hard won inheritance. It is the obligation of all who have inherited it to protect and preserve that freedom and the culture we have created for generations to come, something that is an alien concept to multicultural minds.

It is an article of faith for countless multiculturalists that individualism and individual freedoms are dangerous and that minority group identity is a benign phenomenon. It is the multiculturalist's belief that minority group identity trumps all, including the freedom of speech, because freedom of speech—true freedom of speech—means accepting the right to dissent, no matter what the issue may be, and to hold unorthodox views. At the core of this hard fought freedom is the sentiment expressed by Voltaire's celebrated line, "I disapprove of what you say, but will defend to the death your right to say it."

By contrast, political correctness is profoundly conformist. Its practicioners are very uncomfortable with differing opinions and multiculturalism is the very epitome of political correctness. Suspend reality and pretend that all cultures are equally decent and virtuous, knowing full well this is not true. What could be more politically correct than that?

You can understand why political correctness has been described as a retreat of reason. It grew out of an attitude of decency and consideration towards society's most vulnerable but has become gradually more dogmatic and intolerant of dissent until it now is a betrayal of the very liberal and decent concepts that fueled it in the first place. Political correctness today is less about decency than about image.

And keep this in mind: no aspect of democracy is more anathema to multicultural mentality than free speech because multiculturalism encourages censorship and the condemnation of insensitive utterances—especially utterances that are perceived as potentially offensive to some protected group.

Author George Orwell must have seen this coming when he wrote these famous words: "If liberty means anything at all, it is the freedom to tell people what they do not want to hear." I wonder what multiculturalists would have to say today about Orwell, since to many of them anyone defending freedom of speech is a fanatic!

And I also wonder what Orwell would have to say about the Star Chambers we now call Human Rights Commissions, which are clearly a flagrant violation of free speech. These Commissions have an almost 100 per cent conviction rate because the accusation alone is almost always sufficient to find the defendant guilty. The fact that some individual, or more likely some minority group, found the statement or action to be offensive is proof enough that the accused is guilty and must be punished. These injudicious assaults on democracy and free speech are not only repugnant, but also decidedly un-Canadian. They are a vindictive and outrageous overstepping of government powers.

Because of multiculturalism, hate laws and human rights commissions, minority group culture has become acceptable even though it flies in the face of our beliefs. Reality is superimposed by convoluted language, implausible rhetoric, academic abstraction and a total lack of common sense. Granting any cultural group the ability to circumvent the law by pleading "cultural heritage" is repugnant to most mainstream Canadians.

Obscuring, vague language and obfuscation are the hallmarks of politically correct multiculturalism. We all know not all cultures are equally deserving of our respect and admiration but we mask that knowledge with pious exhortations about accommodation, diversity, and a mass of confusing words that fall upon the facts like a soft snow, blurring the issues and covering all the details.

History students will remember that in the 1930s, Adolph Hitler was admired throughout the world as a proponent of peace because he used all the proper confusing words. Winston Churchill, on the other hand, was branded the warmonger because he spoke bluntly of the truth. Obscure language carried the day.

Remember the lessons learned. Accommodation and appeasement can only result in loss of freedom. Beware!

We are faced today with a titanic struggle between faith and logic. In the Dark Ages, the Catholic Church (faith) demanded the persecution of Galileo (logic and science).

Today, the malignant forces of fundamentalist faith are renewing their strengths from the east and spreading their destructive tentacles ever westward, threatening the Enlightenment (Western values).

Fundamentalist faith can only survive in a dictatorial environment that suppresses all forms of inquiry or dissent.

Science can never survive or thrive under a fundamentalist faith regime because science is naturally curious and has no artificial boundaries. Therefore, fundamentalist faith can only allow technological, and thus economic, stagnation.

Our very way of life will, in all aspects, decline if we remain silent before the threats of minority groups that would silence our inquiries and dissent.

The basic pillar of democratic strength is free speech with no qualifications whatsoever. Hate laws are a hostile reaction to free speech and only support the malignant obfuscation inherent in political correctness.

Free speech is best exemplified by Voltaire's statement that he is prepared to die for it.

It is interesting to note, as well, that it was Alexander Dumas who was sentenced to death by Napoleon III for Dumas' staunch defense of free speech.

How paradoxical that the defense of free speech is a fundamental French tradition that was subverted at a French university in Canada with the cancellation of an address by someone who vigorously questions orthodoxy. (Editor's note: This refers to the cancelled address by Anne Coulter at the University of Ottawa in March, 2010.) It was to be expected, however. Intolerance is the real hallmark of political correctness and multiculturalism.

Wake up, Canada!

– Andy Haydon

Troubled Waters

I think what we are doing to this country is that this idea of multiculturalism has been completely distorted, turned on its head to essentially claim that anything anyone believes—no matter how ridiculous and outrageous it might be—is okay and acceptable in the name of diversity. Where we have gone wrong in this pursuit of multiculturalism is that there is no adherence to core values, the core Canadian values... Sikh extremism is on the rise in some parts of the country and "politically correct" Canadians who let it happen in the name of diversity are partially to blame. We now have second- and third-generation youth whose minds have been poisoned.

(Liberal MP and former NDP Premier of BC Ujjal Dosanjh during an Ottawa press conference, April 21, 2010.)

• • •

Canada doesn't have a culture!

(An angry caller to my show, The Lowell Green Show, 580 CFRA, Ottawa in December 2009, explaining why, after 20 years living in this country, he was sending his children to an Arabic school in Toronto.)

• • •

Canada has lost track of 41,000 illegal immigrants, some of them hardened criminals.

(Auditor General Sheila Fraser in her 2008 report to Parliament.)

• • •

Mahmoud Mohammad Issa Mohammad, a notorious international terrorist who once tossed a grenade amidst the terrified passengers of a hijacked airplane, killing one and wounding many, has been ordered deported from Canada on three separate occasions during the last 23 years but still lives in comfort in Brantford, Ontario.

Canadian Immigration Laws Allow Convicted Terrorist and Killer to Make Home in Ontario

(Steve Brown, Fox News online headline, August 19, 2008.)

• • •

Mihaly Illes is deported from Canada to his native Hungary after being convicted of a string of criminal offences. A few months later he manages to cross back into Canada from the US with the head of a murdered friend stuffed in a Home Depot bucket.

> The Supreme Court of Canada overturned a first-degree murder conviction Friday and ordered a new trial for a Hungarian drug dealer who was in Canada illegally when he was charged with shooting an associate whose severed head was found near Squamish, BC. The ruling gives Mihaly Illes, who slipped back into Canada within months of his 2000 deportation, a fresh chance to clear his name in the 2001 killing of 28-year-old Javan Luke Dowling.

> *(Canwest News Service, October 24, 2008)*

• • •

Everything was at stake—her future marriage, her place in her conservative community, her life. The 23-year-old Muslim woman from the Middle East desperately wanted to appear to be a virgin. She went to Dr. "Sam" with an unusual request. She wanted a hymenoplasty—surgical restoration of the hymen, often done for cosmetic reasons to mimic virginity. "It's a surgery for fooling a person, a lie that the woman is still a virgin, even though she had had sex," said Dr. Faizal Sahukhan, a Burnaby, BC-based sex therapist. He has counselled several South Asian women [in Canada] against seeking the procedure. The procedure is so controversial that most doctors contacted refused to speak about it. Dr. Sam, a doctor in British Columbia's Lower Mainland, only spoke on the condition that his identity be protected for his safety. "There are some people who would not look at this surgery rationally," said Sam who is concerned about retaliation from potentially duped husbands. "The fact is that most of my patients are Muslim…and I'm Jewish and a male."

Sam said he performs the surgery on average twice a month for about $3,500 per procedure, usually on women of Middle Eastern background. One of his clients was preparing for an "arranged marriage" in Oman when she approached him, he said.

"She told me that there is a community doctor who checks to see if the hymen is intact before the marriage," Sam said… He called the correlation between a woman's virginity and her family's honour a "tremendously heavy burden…"

(Tamara Baluja, "Women in Canada seeking controversial 'virginity' surgery," Canwest News Service, July 5, 2010)

• • •

Harjit Singh is ordered deported in 1992 after facing a multitude of charges, including a million-dollar credit card fraud. For 13 years he manages to persuade various appeal boards that he would be tortured if returned to India. It isn't until he claims Liberal Immigration Minister Judy Sgro promised to help him in return for his pizza parlour supplying free pizzas, garlic bread and volunteers for her election campaign that he is finally booted out. In its April 16, 2005, edition, *The Globe and Mail* reports in an article written by Marina Jimenez, entitled "Broken Gates: Canada's welcome mat frayed and unravelling" that, far from being tortured, Harjit Singh is just completing construction of a $300,000 home in an upscale district of Jalandhar. It's estimated his almost one dozen appeals cost Canadian taxpayers several million dollars.

• • •

James Bissett, former head of the Canadian Immigration Service, in a late-2009 interview with me says there are "…tens of thousands of outstanding warrants for the arrest of rejected refugee claimants with little effort being made to enforce the warrants."

• • •

David Harris, former Chief of Strategic Planning for Canadian Security Intelligence Service (CSIS) in a January 2010 call to my radio show in Ottawa claims, "Our immigration and refugee program is a 'death wish.' We cannot possibly properly screen a quarter million immigrants and an additional 30,000 refugees every year." Political correctness carried to the absurd prevents police from issuing descriptions and pictures of even the names of the fugitives. It is the ruling of the courts that it would be an invasion of privacy.

• • •

Hasaka Rathnamalala of the Sri Lankan United National Association of Canada tells the Harper Government that Toronto Tamils are being forced to contribute to the Tamil Tiger cause.

> "There is homegrown terrorism here against people. The collection of money is still going on," said Hasaka Rathnamalala of the Sri Lankan United National Association of Canada, which called a news conference to counter claims of Tamil genocide made last week during a massive demonstration in Toronto.
>
> Rathnamalala said intimidation tactics have included smashed car

windshields, looted homes, computerized identity theft and threats to shut down businesses.

(Lesley Ciarula Taylor, "Group slams Tigers' Toronto 'terrorism,'" Toronto Star, February 4, 2009)

• • •

Although known to be working closely with suspected terrorists, Ahmed Ressam fraudulently obtains a Canadian passport, travels to Afghanistan for explosives training with al Qaeda, returns to Canada, assembles explosives in Montreal and is on his way with them to blow up the Los Angeles airport when a US customs officer catches him. A Seattle judge sentences him to 22 years in prison.

The Terrorist Within, Chapter 4: Sneaking In

(Hal Bernton, Mike Carter, David Heath and James Neff, The Seattle Times, June 23 – July 7, 2002)

• • •

Whether we like it or not, Americans are well aware we have major problems in dealing with terrorists in Canada.

(Martin Collacott, former High Commissioner to Sri Lanka and Maldives and former Ambassador to Cambodia and to Syria and Lebanon and Director for Latin America and Director General for Security Services, personal interview, March 2010.)

• • •

Terrorists and international crime groups are increasingly using Canada as an operational base and transit country en route to the United States. A generous welfare system, lax immigration laws, infrequent prosecutions, light sentencing and long borders and coastlines offer many points of entry that facilitate movements to and from various countries, particularly to the United States.

(A US Congress report issued shortly after 9/11.)

• • •

What the United States sees today when it looks at its northern flank is a neighbor that disregards document fraud, maintains lax visa practices and has the most generous asylum policy in the world. Few asylum seekers are rejected, violators of immigration laws are not vigorously pursued, no one is tracked once inside the country, terrorist groups have the freedom to raise money, criminal enterprises are establishing a secure territorial base and endless litigation negates the law and favors criminals.

(The Center for Immigration Studies, Washington, 2008)

• • •

...the true hidden feature of the organized Islamist effort in Quebec— as in the rest of North America—is to gain acceptance of its agenda. This Islamist effort is highly organized and globally financed. It is multipronged and with an outreach directed to penetrate every level of society from the highest reaches of government to local civic organizations. It is also exceedingly successful in manipulating support for its agenda by reaching out to the "progressives" in the West ever ready to play the role of "useful idiots," as Lenin, the Bolshevic leader, so aptly described them.

In the West, the Islamist agenda is to gain acceptance of Sharia for Muslims to live according to its requirements, and to have western governments adopt some of its directives as with the scheme for Sharia-based finance.

(Salim Mansur, "Taking on Islamists' hidden agenda," QMI Agency, April 24, 2010. Salim Mansur is an Associate Professor of Political Science at Western University, Sun Media columnist and member of the Center for Islamic Pluralism centered in Washington, DC.)

• • •

Clinton Junior Gayle, ordered deported to Jamaica twice previously, is allowed to stay in Canada long enough to shoot and kill Toronto Police Constable Todd Bayliss and seriously wound Constable Mike Leone.

(Radio Station CFRB Toronto, June 17, 1994)

• • •

A franchise of Jamaica's infamous "Shower Posse" has entrenched itself in Toronto, dealing drugs and fuelling internecine gang warfare, according to police who arrested 78 people and seized almost 20 guns in Ontario yesterday.

More than 1,000 police officers from several forces rounded up members of a crime network that allegedly extends from Windsor to Sault Ste. Marie, and even back to Caribbean islands.

A spate of shootings involving feuding gangsters in northwest Toronto drew police interest last August, prompting the nine-month investigation dubbed Project Corral. Several weeks ago, three people—including one with a "cop killer" handgun—were arrested in the Dominican Republic preparing to ship more than 70 kilograms of cocaine to Toronto, police say.

Police say they seized more than $30,000 cash, $10,000 in casino cheques, drugs of all kinds and even diamonds and body armour during the raids.

(Colin Freeze, "Police connect Jamaican Shower Posse to Toronto gangs," The Globe and Mail, *May 5, 2010)*

. . .

The "total fertility rate" [TFRs] in the Arab-Muslim world is the highest in the world and is only exceeded by that of sub-Saharan Africa. The TFRs of a few select countries from the Arab-Muslim world are as follows: Afghanistan, 7.48; Mali, 6.70; Somalia, 6.43; Yemen, 6.02; Palestine territories, 5.63; Iraq, 4.86; Sudan, 4.82; Pakistan, 3.99; Saudi Arabia, 3.81; Jordan, 3.53; Syria, 3.48; Egypt, 3.17 and Bangladesh, 3.22 (United Nations, 2007). This high fertility rate in the Arab-Muslim world has produced a demographic bulge of young people under the age of 25. A high proportion of young men in this age group are unemployed, under-employed, and unemployable due to a lack of education and training for the modern economy.

This reservoir of young males has been estimated to number 25 million by 2010 (Spengler, 2005) and is the source of warriors for the Islamist cause. Many of these young men will migrate to Western countries and there some will join the already existing warriors of Islamist jihad (war) against the citizens and institutions of countries in Europe and North America....

Jihadist wars in Western countries involve not only terrorism but importantly also attacks on existing cultural institutions. For example, Islamists have demanded the creation of a parallel legal system based on Sharia law and changes in existing laws and traditions that interfere with Islamic practices such as unequal relationships between men and women, gender exclusion through dress codes, Islamic tradition of divorce and child custody, non-Western inheritance rules, Sharia financing, polygamy and limits on free speech in discussing Islam. These demands are pushed by Islamist organizations in the West such as the Muslim Council of Britain (MCB), the Council of American–Islamic Relations (CAIR) in the United States and its counterpart or subsidiary in Canada (CAIR-Can), the Islamic Society of North America (ISNA), the Canadian Islamic Congress (CIC), the Muslim Student Associations (MSA) and a host of others....

(Salim Mansur, The Effects of Mass Immigration on Canadian Living Standards and Society, *published by the Fraser Institute, August 2009.)*

• • •

Allegations of an anti-Semitic outburst at York University drew condemnation yesterday from the Jewish community amid concerns of mounting hostility on the school's campus.

The university's Hillel student group contends its members were intimidated following a news conference on Wednesday.

Hillel and other organizations held the event to call for the ouster of the York Federation of Students' executive, who backed the school's teaching assistants during the recent 12-week strike.

Representatives of the student federation, along with members of Students Against the Israeli Apartheid (SAIA), a pro-Palestinian group, disrupted the news conference with chants of "Zionism is racism" and "Shame on Hillel," according to Daniel Ferman, Hillel's president.

The press conference was shut down, but the same group of students later pursued Mr. Ferman and other participants in the press conference to Hillel's Lounge in York's student centre. Approximately 100 people swarmed outside the lounge, taunting the students inside and threatening to break the glass, Mr. Ferman said. "We basically kept our students inside—it was mostly Jewish students but there were non-Jewish students too," he said. "We were basically held hostage in our own space."

Mr. Ferman says he was also referred to as a "dirty Jew" and "f—ing Jew" by members of the throng.

The students inside the lounge called for help and were eventually escorted off campus by university security and police.

(James Cowan, "York Jewish students claim intimidation," National Post, *February 12, 2009)*

• • •

A secessionist Tamil government-in-exile, with the largest block made up of Canadian Tamils will not improve the life of their brethren in Sri

Lanka and will only succeed in impeding that country's ability to re-build after its recent bloody history. Rather than relive old battles, Canada's Tamil diaspora should support peace and reconciliation in their homeland. Otherwise, Toronto, home to half of Canada's esti-mated 200,000 Sri Lankans risks becoming a base for disaffected members of the Liberation Tigers of Tamil Eelam, the group that fought for a quarter century for an independent homeland.

(Editorial, "Head off the phantom Tigers' Canadian base," The Globe and Mail, May 18, 2010)

. . .

A Canadian who was being investigated for allegedly joining a Somali militant group died in a "fierce battle" according to a eulogy posted on an extremist website.

Mohammed Elmi Ibrahim, 22, was one of a half-dozen radicalized young Somali-Canadians who allegedly left Toronto last year to join the al-Qaeda-linked Al-Shabab.

Members of Canada's large Somali community say they are worried that some youths are being radicalized by al Shabab propaganda on the Internet.

(Stewart Bell, "Extremists praise Somali Canadian in online eulogy," National Post, May 4, 2010)

. . .

Canada has become the world's number one hotel!

(Bestselling author Yann Martel)

• • •

The Changing Face of Canada: As minority population booms, a visible majority emerges.

(The Globe and Mail, March 10, 2010)

• • •

With the scars of the Air India bombing still fresh, the BC premier and most other politicians boycott the April 17, 2010, Vaisakhi parade in Surrey after organizers warn politicians they might not be safe if they attend.

One of those threatened, Liberal MP Ujjal Dosanjh, says the Surrey Vaisakhi parade, marking the birth of Sikhism, contains extremist rhetoric, violent portraits and separatist slogans. In 2008, the Indian government formally complained to Canada that the parade depicted the assassins of Indira Gandhi as martyrs. The Surrey parade is the largest of its kind outside India with some 120,000 lining the streets and this year featuring a float honouring Sikh martyrs—including members of separatist groups in India that the Canadian government has branded as terrorist organizations.

Vaisakhi parade risky for MP Ujjal Dosanjh and MLA Dave Hayer: organizer. Pair told to avoid Surrey Sikh festival.

(*Lori Culbert and Jonathan Fowlie*, Vancouver Sun, *April 16, 2010*)

• • •

Multiculturalism teaches that all cultures and religions are equally worthy of respect, except Christianity and whiteness.

(*Columnist Barbara Kay*, "*It's not all good*," National Post, *April 28, 2010*)

• • •

More than 100 Sikhs engage in a bloody fight inside the Sri Guru Nanak Sikh Temple in Brampton on the quiet Sunday afternoon of April 18, 2010. Hammers, knives and machetes slash and hack. Five are hospitalized. It's a fight over who controls the temple, say police. Two weeks earlier, only about a kilometre away, Manjit Mangat, a prominent Brampton lawyer, was stabbed outside the Sikh Lehar Temple by two men brandishing kirpans, the ceremonial dagger worn by baptized Sikhs.

The bloody melee that consumed a Toronto-area Sikh temple this past weekend is evidence of a bitter control struggle consuming its leadership, observers say—and the trouble is not unique.

Jagdish Grewal, editor of the Canadian Punjabi Post, says separatists—those who back an independent Sikh state called Khalistan—maintain control of many large temples in Canada and bring with them a legacy of "muscle power."

Late last year, Mr. Grewal was held at gunpoint and attacked by three masked men outside the newspaper offices in Brampton.

(Megan O'Toole, "Tensions at Sikh temple not unique," National Post, *April 20, 2010)*

• • •

Surely by now we have received enough signals that something is seriously wrong with the way we are going about the integration of newcomers to Canada. And surely the time has come when Canadians should put aside the political correctness that has inhibited us from taking a close look at extremism that is incubating right under our noses.

(Immigration expert Martin Collacott, personal interview, March 2010)

• • •

"In Vancouver and Toronto, the Asian influence is very evident. That will put us in a unique position compared to other world cities. As we look towards the 'Pacific Century'… Vancouver is the first Asian city outside of Asia." [says] Tung Chan, CEO of S.U.C.C.E.S.S., an organization helping immigrants to Canada.

(Joe Friesen, "The changing face of Canada: As minority population booms, a visible majority emerges," The Globe and Mail, *March 10, 2010)*

• • •

Heading for Disaster

If you listen carefully, you can hear the waves crashing on the nearby reef. Disaster looms ever closer. As a nation, we're still afloat, the spirit is still alive, all is not yet lost. But, if we don't get this ship of state turned around, we will surely run aground and tear ourselves apart on the jagged rocks of mass immigration and multiculturalism, lured ever closer to the lurking danger of cultural suicide by the siren call of political correctness.

I don't believe most Canadians really understand the dangerous situation we are placing ourselves in. But it's not too late. Before we talk about solutions, we've got to fully comprehend the problems we face. Until I began to thoroughly research our immigration and multiculturalism policies and their ramifications, I had no idea of the extent of the damage we are doing to ourselves and to our country and no idea of the disaster that lies just ahead if we don't swiftly change course.

It's not as though there are no warnings. Events in the Netherlands, Britain, Denmark, France, and elsewhere in Europe stand like modern-day lighthouses signalling danger.

Do not come this way. Stay away from these rocks. Drop anchor. Steer clear. Just off your bow are uncharted shoals you may not successfully navigate.

Incredibly, many of those on watch can't see the reef or don't recognize it for the peril it presents. They cannot or will not hear the crashing sounds of furious waters dead ahead. "We're headed for a new country," they tell us. "A new Canada. Oh, happy day!"

New Canada

Since 1945, Canada has received about ten million immigrants of diverse origins. I believe this ongoing mass immigration is causing Canada to evolve into a diasporatic society. Canada is becoming a home away from home for a range of peoples whose identities are rooted not in Canada, but in countries and regions of origin. In other words, Canada is evolving into a global suburb.

Although Canada's policy of mass immigration raises many important issues there is a strange absence of national political or public debate on the subject. Debate should normally be expected to arise on such issues as the number of immigrants allowed into Canada annually, their real impact on Canada's society and economy, the identity and meaning of Canada in a situation of growing diversity and potentially lessening social cohesion. In fact, however, these questions have not been the subject of major public discussion and little effort has been made to consider what Canada will look like 20, 50 or 100 years in the future.

(Dr. Stephen Gallagher, The Effects of Mass Immigration on Canadian Living Standards and Society, *published by the Fraser Institute, August 2009. Dr. Gallagher is Program Director of the Montreal Branch of the Canadian International Council and a lecturer in Political Science. He has taught at McGill University, Carleton University and the University of Manitoba.)*

• • •

The problem is, of course, in order to arrive at "New Canada" we must scrap "Old Canada" and is that really what we want to do? Is it really what we *should* do? And if so, why?

Those who espouse this glorious "New Canada" have never clearly explained exactly why "Old Canada" should be scuttled. What national faults are so grave as to justify a cultural death sentence? Nor has anyone explained to us what kind of improvements we can expect to see with this glorious "New Canada."

Will "New Canada" have nicer, more generous people? Will our politicians be more honest? Will our taxes be lower? Will our hockey players stop taking head shots at their opponents? Will childbirth be less painful? Will our drivers stop tailgating? Will there be less crime? Fewer fires? Will kids stop talking back to their parents? Will grandparents have fewer aches and pains? Will those ordered deported actually be compelled to leave? Please tell us, how much better off will we all be in "New Canada?" Will we all be happier? Safer? Richer? More content?

Because if we won't be better off, if we won't all be happier, then what's the sense of destroying the old if we're not going to replace it with a new, *improved* model?

And could someone please inform us exactly what kind of damage will be done to "Old Canada" during this marvellous transformation? Will we be left with anything our ancestors created for us? Will we be allowed to retain anything of our heritage? Can we at least keep hockey or will soccer take over entirely? And, oh yes, this question: What is all this going to cost us at a time when they're closing down operating rooms in our hospitals for lack of funds? How will we pay for this glorious metamorphosis?

Of course, we've got to understand when the self-anointed "progressives" talk about "New Canada" they're really talking about you and me. Not the landscape! Not the flora and fauna! We, the people, have got to smarten up, they tell us. We've got to get "progressive" like they are and understand that we really don't have a culture in Canada worth saving. At least, not in English Canada.

"Old Canada's" culture, they insist, doesn't cut the mustard anymore. We've got to import a few dozen other cultures, all of which, they insist, must have equal status. Laws are passed to ensure that any attempt to create one dominant culture is illegal. We cannot have a common national culture in English Canada.

No distinct Canadian culture for us, but a really nice heaping basketful of other cultures, including some that most of us aren't too crazy about.

Except for Quebec, of course. Quebec has a real culture, we've been told since Prime Minister Pierre Trudeau's time. The only culture in the country worth protecting. And heaven only knows we've invested billions of dollars and tons of sweat and worry doing just that—protecting Quebec's culture. And will continue so doing!

Please understand, to the casual observer "New Canada" will look pretty much the same as "Old Canada." The Rockies will still be there. So, too, the Prairies, the Great Lakes, the St. Lawrence. Oh, I suppose some of the store signs in places like Toronto, Vancouver, Ottawa and Montreal will look a little different. They may change a few street names, but I'm pretty sure they won't be moving the Parliament Buildings or the CN Tower. The Toronto Maple Leafs will still be—well, the Leafs—so at least that part of our culture won't change. (Let's hope!)

The Evolution

Thanks to Statistics Canada, we have a pretty good idea how "New Canada" is going to evolve.

First of all, we are told, over the next 20 years the foreign-born population of "New Canada" will grow four times faster than those who are born in this country.

When you examine the numbers I bring to light in this book, you will see that we don't have to wait 20 years for this to occur. The foreign-born population of Canada is growing at least four times faster than those born here right now; indeed I suspect the rate is probably closer to five times faster. No speculation is involved in this fact; it comes directly from Statistics Canada, which tells us that by 2031 at least one in four people in the country will have been born elsewhere, and only about half of all working-age people will belong to families that have lived in Canada for at least three generations.

We know a few other things about "New Canada" as well, once again courtesy of Statistics Canada. For example, by 2031 one-third of all people living here will be so-called visible minorities—minorities, that is, until very quickly those with Western values become the minority "race," something that will surely occur within the lifetime of many of you reading this.

Something else we know is that in "New Canada" more than 70 per cent of all immigrants flooding into the country will make a beeline for one of three cities: Toronto, Vancouver and, to a lesser extent, Montreal.

By that magic year 2031, fully 63 per cent of Toronto's population will be visible minorities—in Vancouver the ratio will be 59 per cent, in Montreal 31 per cent. Ottawa's visible minorities population will increase from the present 19 per cent to 36 per cent.

Visible minorities in Canada, 2031

Projected percentage of non-Caucasian population in Census metropolitan areas.

Top 10	2006	2031
Toronto	43%	63%
Vancouver	42%	59%
Abbotsford, BC	23%	39%
Calgary	22%	38%
Ottawa	19%	36%
Windsor	16%	33%
Montreal	16%	31%
Edmonton	17%	29%
Kitchener	14%	28%
Winnipeg	15%	27%
Bottom 5		
Moncton	2%	5%
St. John's	2%	5%
Sudbury	2%	5%
Trois-Rivières	2%	4%
Saguenay	1%	2%

Source: Statistics Canada

It is important to realize that we are doing something in Canada no other nation on earth even contemplates. This country today is undergoing a societal and demographic evolution that is much more rapid and profound than is taking place in any other nation on earth. For example, while only ten per cent of Americans today are foreign-born, here in Canada the foreign-born figure is about 20 per cent. While some US cities have large foreign-born populations, none of them approach what is occurring in Toronto and Vancouver. Americans often joke that Miami's first language is Spanish, but in fact only about 36 per cent of its population was born outside the United States, compared to nearly 46 per cent of Toronto's population and almost 40 per cent in Vancouver in 2006.

The significance of this is even greater since Toronto and Vancouver are by far the largest cities in English Canada and pretty well determine which political party governs the country.

So "New Canada" will in fact be two Canadas. The really, really "New Canada" in Toronto, Vancouver, Montreal and Ottawa and the pretty much status-quo-Canada in the rest of the country, at least for the time being. On second thought, when you factor Quebec into the equation, "New Canada" will actually be three Canadas.

This, we are assured by the great "progressive" thinkers of the land, is a good thing. Not a problem! There is no treacherous reef waiting just off our bow to tear us apart, they promise.

Any expressions of concern that mass immigration and multicul-turalism are threatening our core values or diluting our national character are dismissed as the drooling rants of a few old white guys whose diapers are beginning to chafe! Furthermore, they claim any-one suggesting that maybe "Old Canada" is a pretty decent place that doesn't deserve to be deep-sixed is probably just a racist.

Who's The Racist?

Former New York Mayor Rudy Giuliani says a "policy of political correctness" has led to missed signals in recent terrorism investigations.

(Giuliani responding to questions concerning the failed attempt to detonate a car bomb in Times Square, ABC News, "This Week" on May 9, 2010.)

No doubt some of the objections and concerns being expressed about "New Canada" *are* coming from old white guys. Quite likely some of it comes from bona fide racists as well.

But wait just a minute here.

Those who revel at the prospect of a Toronto with a 63 per cent visible minority population very clearly believe that the fewer white faces around the better.

dream come true for most of those on Canada's political left. A dream that, according to Statistics Canada, will be realized in Toronto and Vancouver within the next dozen years or so!

In fact, the latest Census figures (2006) show that five million, or 18.4 per cent of Canada's population, is comprised of visible minorities, and that an astonishing 60 per cent of these live in just two cities—Toronto and Vancouver. Metro Toronto's foreign-born population in 2006 was 46 per cent while Metro Vancouver had almost 40 per cent foreign-born residents. Please understand—we're talking people not born in this country soon becoming the majority in English Canada's two largest cities.

It is important to note that, in his later years, Trudeau admitted that one of his great disappointments was that his multicultural policies didn't help different groups celebrate and integrate their particular diversities within the common universality of the Canadian experience but rather resulted in nothing more than ever-growing demands for financial entitlements from those groups.

Whether he grew concerned over the growing tidal wave of non-Europeans into Canada, we will never know. However, if you examine his record, you will see that he was extremely protective of Quebec's language and culture.

Don't forget, on February 20, 1978, then-Prime Minister Trudeau, signed into law what is called the *Cullen-Couture Agreement* giving Quebec the sole responsibility for determining the number of immigrants allowed into that province, the selection of those immigrants, their reception and their integration.

The agreement states: "…in order to provide Quebec with new means to preserve its demographic importance in Canada and to ensure the integration of immigrants in Quebec in a manner that respects the distinct identity of Quebec…." And so, Quebec has the rights and responsibilities set out in writing with respect to the number of immigrants, the selection and integration.

The agreement even spells out Quebec's rights in more detail, stating emphatically: "Quebec has sole responsibility for the selection of Immigrants destined to that province…."

No other province has similar rights.

Thus it is that the law protects Quebec's language and culture while the rest of Canadian culture is deemed not worthy of preservation.

What's Happening to Our Two Official Languages?

As further clarification of what's happening in our country, let's examine the languages we are importing.

Here are a few figures that must have Trudeau spinning in his grave wondering what ever happened to his idea of bilingualism:

The total number of immigrants allowed into Canada in 2008 was 247,243, not including refugees denied citizenship but who remain here, and not counting temporary workers or foreign students, many of whom also remain in Canada for many years.

Believe it or not, only 11.2 per cent of that number had English as their mother tongue, and only 3.8 per cent listed French as their mother tongue.

Let's have a brief look at the raw numbers from 1999 until 2008:

Canada—Permanent residents by mother tongue

Mother Tongue	1999	2000	2001	2002	2003	2004	2005	2006	2007	2008
English	18,606	19,560	22,136	18,868	18,694	22,032	22,906	24,884	26,615	28,751
Mandarin	24,975	31,389	36,178	28,127	31,714	31,456	37,321	28,049	23,207	26,086
Arabic	12,496	15,492	20,217	18,049	17,218	18,985	19,516	20,008	18,996	21,925
Tagalog	8,328	9,612	12,557	10,610	11,442	12,443	16,332	16,099	16,539	20,835
Spanish	7,250	8,719	10,143	10,461	12,489	14,319	17,106	17,059	16,913	16,292
Punjabi	11,396	14,038	14,402	15,270	13,845	13,256	17,037	17,714	14,281	14,315
French	4,722	5,343	5,597	5,199	5,391	6,802	7,476	7,430	8,305	8,334
Urdu	8,616	13,613	15,250	13,466	11,960	11,722	12,798	11,231	8,896	7,899
Korean	7,236	7,661	9,664	7,410	7,179	5,420	5,905	6,295	5,983	7,377
Russian	9,349	9,449	10,017	9,416	8,392	8,759	8,637	7,300	7,293	6,697
Chinese	9,927	8,761	7,113	6,768	4,412	4,656	5,743	6,114	5,230	5,693
Farsi	4,653	4,502	4,680	6,916	5,042	5,069	4,936	6,117	5,838	5,459
Hindi	2,937	4,303	5,339	5,320	4,395	5,347	6,017	5,220	4,604	4,615
Tamil	5,150	6,480	6,195	5,825	4,915	5,113	5,318	5,237	4,292	4,492
Gujarati	2,039	5,316	5,463	5,964	4,731	4,656	7,363	5,615	5,183	4,193
German	2,207	2,201	1,961	1,866	2,245	2,387	2,565	3,077	2,864	4,144
Romanian	3,542	4,541	5,628	5,815	5,559	5,859	5,261	4,877	4,494	3,536
Cantonese	5,451	5,322	4,704	5,243	5,207	5,008	5,452	4,677	3,977	3,434
Bengali	2,357	3,495	4,414	3,517	2,498	3,158	4,656	4,411	3,271	3,370
Creole	1,516	1,786	2,693	2,415	2,386	2,254	2,252	1,956	1,989	3,142
Portuguese	1,015	1,311	1,461	1,229	1,259	1,424	1,540	1,730	2,197	2,856
Other african languages	555	727	720	1,125	2,375	3,512	3,250	2,781	2,452	2,187
Other Southeast Asia languages	691	572	617	403	507	702	742	1,093	1,479	2,100
Vietnamese	1,412	1,782	2,058	2,164	1,709	1,814	1,872	3,062	2,540	1,915
Dari	1,613	2,240	2,705	2,659	2,499	2,062	2,383	2,265	1,868	1,599
Top 25 languages	158,039	188,215	211,912	194,105	188,063	198,215	224,384	214,301	199,306	211,246
Other languages	31,915	39,243	38,727	34,944	33,285	37,610	37,857	37,342	37,448	35,997
Total	189,954	227,458	250,639	229,049	221,348	235,825	262,241	251,643	236,754	247,243

Source: *Immigration Overview, Permanent and Temporary Residents*, Immigration Canada

Canada—Permanent residents by mother tongue, percentage distribution

Mother Tongue	1999	2000	2001	2002	2003	2004	2005	2006	2007	2008
English	10.1	9.8	8.6	8.8	8.2	8.5	9.3	8.7	9.9	11.2
Mandarin	10.7	13.2	13.8	14.4	12.3	14.3	13.3	14.2	11.2	9.8
Arabic	6.6	6.6	6.8	8.1	7.9	7.8	8.1	7.4	8.0	8.0
Tagalog	3.7	3.8	3.8	4.1	4.6	5.6	6.1	6.5	6.8	7.1
Spanish	4.4	4.4	4.2	5.0	4.6	5.2	5.3	6.2	6.4	7.0
Punjabi	6.2	6.0	6.2	5.8	6.7	6.3	5.6	6.5	7.0	6.0
French	4.6	4.5	6.0	6.1	5.9	5.4	5.0	4.9	4.5	3.8
Urdu	2.6	2.5	2.4	2.2	2.3	2.4	2.9	2.9	3.0	3.5
Korean	6.3	4.9	4.2	4.0	4.1	3.8	3.7	3.3	2.9	3.1
Russian	2.9	3.8	3.4	3.9	3.2	3.2	2.3	2.3	2.5	2.5
Chinese	3.2	2.5	2.0	1.9	3.0	2.3	2.2	1.9	2.4	2.5
Farsi	4.7	5.2	3.9	2.0	3.0	2.0	2.0	2.2	2.4	2.2
Hindi	1.1	1.1	2.3	2.2	2.6	2.1	2.0	2.8	2.2	2.2
Tamil	1.2	1.6	1.9	2.1	2.3	2.0	2.3	2.3	2.1	2.0
Gujarati	1.8	1.9	2.0	2.3	2.5	2.5	2.5	2.0	1.9	1.9
German	2.2	2.7	2.9	2.5	2.5	2.2	2.2	2.0	2.1	1.8
Romanian	5.9	2.9	2.3	1.9	2.3	2.4	2.1	2.1	1.9	1.7
Cantonese	1.3	1.2	1.5	1.8	1.5	1.1	1.3	1.8	1.8	1.4
Bengali	1.1	1.2	1.0	0.8	0.8	1.0	1.0	1.0	1.2	1.2
Creole	0.9	0.7	0.8	0.8	0.9	0.8	0.8	0.7	1.2	1.1
Portuguese	0.3	0.3	0.3	0.3	0.5	1.1	1.5	1.2	1.1	1.0
Other African languages	0.6	0.5	0.6	0.6	0.5	0.6	0.6	0.6	0.7	0.9
Other Southeast Asia languages	0.8	0.8	0.8	1.1	1.1	1.1	1.0	0.9	0.8	0.8
Vietnamese	0.8	0.9	1.0	1.1	1.2	1.1	0.9	0.9	0.9	0.8
Dari	0.0	0.1	0.1	0.1	0.1	0.1	0.1	0.1	0.4	0.8
Top 5 languages	84.0	82.9	82.5	84.4	84.6	84.9	83.8	85.4	85.1	84.3
Other languages	16.0	17.1	17.5	15.7	15.4	15.2	16.2	14.6	14.9	15.7
Total	100.0	100.0	100.0	100.0	100.0	100.0	100.0	100.0	100.0	100.0

Source: *Immigration Overview, Permanent and Temporary Residents*, Immigration Canada

To sum up:

- Total immigrants entering Canada in 2008 with French or English as their mother tongue: 37,085.

- Total with language other than French or English as their mother tongue: 210,158.

- Total percentage with English or French as their mother tongue: 15.

- Percentage of new Canadians arriving in 2008 with neither of our two official languages as their mother tongue: 84.5.

Very clearly, in 2008 the number of immigrants whose mother tongue was neither English nor French outnumbered those from English- or French-speaking nations almost SEVEN TO ONE!

That is not so say, of course, that some of those with mother tongues other than French or English cannot speak one or both of our official languages, but the figures do provide a very graphic idea of just where most modern-day immigrants are coming from—certainly not French- or English-speaking nations. And, please keep in mind that the majority of French-speaking immigrants come to Quebec.

By 2031, according to the latest figures from Statistics Canada, fully 25 per cent of Canada's population will be foreign born and, as we can easily see from the previous charts, there is a very good chance fewer than half of them will be able to speak either one of our official languages. No other country in the world is faced with that situation, a situation of our own making.

Are we absolutely certain we should be doing this? Is this really what you want? Because if this isn't the Canada you want, you better speak up now before it's just too late. There is a point of no return, and I suspect we're approaching it very rapidly.

That dangerous reef isn't over the horizon anymore; it's in full view.

In fairness, while it is true that Trudeau sprang multiculturalism on us in 1971, it was at a time when immigration was mostly from European nations. It is doubtful he envisioned a day when the "multi" cultures from non-European nations would outnumber Europeans about four, five or even seven to one. That lovely little gift, as we have already noted, is courtesy of Mulroney and Chrétien. Although, to be honest, every government since, including that of Stephen Harper, continues along the same dangerous path.

Harper has taken some steps to tighten up our refugee system, which I will discuss later in this book, but the approximately four-to-one ratio of non-Europeans to Europeans continues at the same rate it has for the past two decades. If anything, the ratio of non-Europeans to Europeans continues to increase, as we can see from the language numbers. Fewer immigrants are arriving from Western nations every year while the rate of immigration remains virtually constant.

We've Always Been Multiracial

Something that seems lost to most politicians and journalists is that Canada has always been a multiracial country. If you have another look at the chart on page 50 you will easily see that until the early 1990s we opened our doors to the beleaguered citizens of dozens of European countries, all of which had and have very divergent cultures. The Scots brought their kilts, the Germans their lederhosen, the French their croissants, the Irish their songs, and together they overcame tremendous obstacles to create a wonderful open and free culture. A proud nation of hard-working, law-abiding, innovative, honest and brave people. They created Canada!

Of course, we welcomed immigrants from non-European countries. They flocked here by the thousands from India, Pakistan, China, Lebanon and the Philippines; they prospered along with everyone else prepared to work hard. In many cases, they actually prospered better than Canadians born here.

But always we made sure that the European nature of the land remained intact. For every non-European who settled here we made sure at least four came from Europe or the US. We welcomed those from other lands, but we had no intention of turning any of our cities into a Canadian China, a Canadian India or Canadian Pakistan.

The Chinese, after all, left China to come to Canada, not to China and the East Indians left India for Canada not for India but, as we can see here, all of that changed, first under Trudeau with his multicultural policies and then Brian Mulroney and Jean Chrétien, who opened the floodgates to non-Europeans.

It was all three of them who decided, on our behalf, that English Canada didn't have a culture worth preserving so they very kindly provided a new culture for us—a "New Canada."

We never had a say in it. We were never asked. It was never debated in Parliament. Those three men and their cabinets decided for purely political reasons to change the very nature and culture of this county. It wasn't done with the best interests of Canada at heart. In fact, one wonders if any of them spent a minute worrying what it would do to this country. It was done purely for one thing—votes. Ethnic votes.

Please note one thing. One important thing. All three—Trudeau, Mulroney and Chrétien—came from Quebec, which got to keep, and even enhance, its culture.

It was only English Canada whose culture was to be yanked from under it and replaced with something entirely foreign. Only English Canada didn't have a culture worth saving.

Sadly, most of us really didn't realize what was happening and bought the whole thing—hook, line and sinker!

Did Europeans Stop Liking Us?

How could immigration source patterns change so suddenly? Was it planned or accidental? Why would immigration from the UK and Europe just suddenly dry up? Is it because people from those nations woke up one morning and decided they liked it just fine where they were and didn't want to leave? Or was it a deliberate attempt on the part of government and immigration officials to dilute the primarily European-Judeo-Christian culture that has served Canada so well over the years? And if it was deliberate, why?

I put these questions and others to the Canadian who is perhaps the best qualified of all to provide an unbiased response—Martin Collacott, who worked more than 30 years with the Canadian Department of External Affairs and served as Director General for Security Services responsible for the coordination of counterterrorism at the international level. In addition, Collacott is a former High Commissioner to Sri Lanka and Maldives and a former Ambassador to Cambodia and to Syria and Lebanon. Among his responsibilities was the administration of our immigration and refugee policies. As further evidence of Collacott's qualifications, he was the Chinese-speaking member of Canada's negotiating team that established diplomatic relations with China.

In Collacott's opinion, as expressed to me, this seemingly sudden switch from mostly European immigration to mostly non-European was not a deliberate attempt to literally change the face of Canada, but was rather the "unintended consequences of decisions made in the 1960s." That was the time the Government decided to refine our immigration policy to attract more highly skilled and better-educated immigrants. Instead of hewers of wood and fetchers of water, we decided to aim a little higher and attract more professionals, business people and entrepreneurs.

"The decision was also made," Collacott told me, "that it didn't matter where the immigrants came from."

One of the consequences of this was that it attracted large numbers of skilled and well-educated Asians, while discouraging the inflow of less-skilled workers from Europe. Suddenly bringing family members to Canada from the UK and Europe became much more difficult.

According to Collacott, this worked out very well for a while. "Then," he told me, "the trouble started when many of these new Canadians from non-European countries became settled in their communities and decided what was really missing were relatives. It was at that point that immigration changed from what's best for Canada and became a political ploy. Large numbers of family members flocked to our shores as the 'Family Class' category was greatly extended. That's when an increasing number of immigrants with few, if any, skills required in this country began to strain our social programs, in particular health care and education." (Immigration skyrocketed from 71,698 in 1961 to more than 222,876 in 1967.)

"But," added Collacott, "at least in the 1960s and '70s we had the wits to adjust our intake of immigrants to match economic conditions. Trudeau, for example, lowered immigration substantially in the early part of the 1980s to adjust to the severe recession we were enduring." (Immigration dropped from 218,416 in 1974 to 143,140 in 1980 then continued in free fall until it bottomed out at 84,346 in 1985.)

Enter Barbara McDougall, leading the "red" Tories under Conservative Prime Minister Brian Mulroney.

According to Collacott, it was McDougall who, as the Minister of Employment and Immigration, convinced Mulroney and her Cabinet colleagues in 1990 that we should raise immigration levels to 250,000 a year and sustain very high rates of immigration as a means to capture the ethnic vote and stay in power.

This claim is also advanced by James Bissett, former Canadian Ambassador to Yugoslavia, Bulgaria and Albania, former High Commissioner to Trinidad and Tobago, and from 1985 until 1990, Executive Director of the Canadian Immigration Service.

In the landmark book entitled *The Effects of Mass Immigration on*

Canadian Living Standards and Society, published by the Fraser Institute, Bissett writes:

> Until the mid-1980s, the immigration movement to Canada was regulated in accordance with economic conditions. When there was a buoyant economy and a strong demand for labour, the intake was increased; at times of economic down-turn and rising unemployment, the tap was turned off and immigration was reduced. This was the system that had governed the flow of immigrants since the end of the Second World War and it had served Canada and the immigrants well.
>
> However in 1985 the newly elected Progressive Conservative government of Prime Minister Brian Mulroney raised immigration levels despite evidence of an economic down-turn. This was the signal that the Conservative party was determined to win ethnic votes by supporting high immigration levels. In 1990, the then [Immigration] Minister, Barbara McDougall, convinced her cabinet colleagues to raise the levels to 250,000, by arguing that higher levels would help the Party to establish stronger ties with ethnic communities. Later, the Minister said in an interview that a political party was not doing its job if it failed to reach out to ethnic groups (Windsor, 1990, October 24). There was political capital to be gained by high numbers whether they were needed or not.

The decision had already been made that it didn't matter where the immigrants were coming from. Just pack as many into the country as we can and make sure they all vote for us! Bissett continues:

> This change in policy marked a significant turning point in the way the immigration program was to be managed in the years ahead. The

numbers to be admitted were no longer to be governed primarily by economic factors.

This was made abundantly clear during the just now concluding "Great Recession" when, despite an unemployment rate near nine per cent, immigration levels remained as high and even went up from where they were during the boom days at the turn of the century. Bissett goes on to say:

> Immigration has become politicized, and immigrants were to be seen by all political parties as potential voters. The two political parties that have subsequently shared power now compete with each other in raising the immigration levels and even the New Democratic Party advocates higher levels. Numbers have become the primary consideration.

This view is also held by Daniel Stoffman, co-author of *Boom, Bust and Echo*, one of the bestselling books in Canadian history. Stoffman's expertise in immigration dates back to 1991 when he was awarded an Atkinson Fellowship in Public Policy to produce a background paper on the matter for the C.D. Howe Institute.

In his book *Who Gets In: What's wrong with Canada's immigration program—and how to fix it* Stoffman writes:

> Annual intake, which used to fluctuate according to economic conditions, was raised under Mulroney to unprecedented levels and made permanent. In the earlier system, intake was adjusted according to the absorptive capacity of the economy and labour market conditions.

> The policy of permanent high immigration, instituted by Mulroney

and carried on by Chrétien, is unique in the world. It puts needless stress on both the host society and the most recent newcomers themselves whose entry to the Canadian economy is made more difficult by the need to compete with a relentless flow of new immigrants.

No real attempt was made to bring our runaway immigration system under some control until Bill C-50 was approved by Parliament in February 2008 and passed into law June 17, 2008. This new law, which by the way was fought tooth and nail by all three opposition parties, places greater emphasis on admitting immigrants who have the skills required at specific times in Canada. Ongoing consultations with the provinces to determine exactly what skills are required now and in the foreseeable future are still under way across the country.

Whether in fact these changes to the *Immigration and Refugee Protection Act* (IRPA) will curb the tidal wave of immigration is doubtful.

In the first place, the new system does not apply to all those who are already in the long lineup waiting to immigrate to Canada. The waiting list will have to be dealt with first and, believe it or not, as of June 17, 2008, when the Senate approved the changes, there were an unbelievable 925,000 people on that list, some of whom had been waiting six years for decisions on their applications.

Had Bill C-50 not been passed, it is estimated the waiting list would have grown to 1.5 million by the end of 2011.

One of the obvious problems with huge waiting lists is that an employer may put in an "order" for, let's say, a dozen welders, but by the time they're plucked out of the lineup, three, four or even five years will likely have gone by. Hardly of any benefit to anyone, including the prospective immigrant.

If we continue bringing in immigrants and refugees at the rate of close to 300,000 per year, it will take more than three years just to clear the backlog. Only then can the new rules come into effect and there's a very good chance we will have a change of government by that time.

If the Liberals are returned there is every indication they will revert to wide-open immigration since, at the time of its approval, they opposed Bill C-50. (If the bill had been defeated, it would have triggered a non-confidence motion, possibly bringing down the Harper government. This was avoided by a number of Liberals absenting themselves from the vote in the House.)

As of the publication of this book, there is no indication of any slowing in the number of immigrants pouring into Canada.

Despite what some say is the worst recession since the "Dirty Thirties," the goal last year (2009), as stated by Citizenship and Immigration Canada, was to accept between 240,000 and 265,000 new permanent residents, including approximately 70,000 in the family class. In addition, 33,200 refugees sought sanctuary in Canada last year, most of whom will be here for years. Factor in at least another quarter of a million who entered under temporary worker status, plus close to 70,000 foreign students, and you are dealing with a situation that, as Stoffman says, cannot be sustained.

Stoffman goes on to say:

> Few understand the extent of the damage inflicted on it [our immigration policy] by Brian Mulroney and Jean Chrétien. The damage is three-fold; the number of immigrants admitted annually is too high; the proportion of skilled immigrants it too low; and the refugee determination system cannot distinguish between real refugees and fraudulent ones.

Few Canadians are fully aware of all the benefits available to those who declare refugee status in this country. Benefits that go far beyond anything available in any other country in the world. Refugee claimants here in Canada are free to work at whatever job they can find, they can collect full welfare benefits, and obtain free health and dental care. They are also eligible for free housing and free legal services, something they quickly learn if they have not already been apprised of all of this before setting foot in Canada. Not only that, but according to Stoffman, almost all refugee claimants up until the past couple years have been accepted as landed immigrants, which allows them to stay here permanently and bring in a whole raft of relatives.

The Self-Loathers

What Stoffman does not deal with, at least not head-on, is the matter of the "New Canada" that is being created for us. The new and improved Canada that will very soon see an end to the domination of a Euro-Judeo-Christian culture that has served this country so well.

Stoffman comes about as close to the heart of the matter as I suspect he dares when he talks about what he describes as the "cultural left."

> It [the cultural left] wants more immigration because it loathes the culture of the Canadian majority, people of British, French and other European origins. The "cultural left" looks forward to the day when non-European are dominant!

Obviously the "cultural left," as described by Stoffman, are going to be jumping for joy very soon.

A View From Britain

Interestingly enough, this argument that many of those on the left, (or as Stoffman describes them "the cultural left") loathe Western societies is a key theme in another bestselling book about another country's dangerous immigration policies.

Melanie Phillips, author of the book that took Britain by storm, *Londonistan*, had an article published in 2006 in the *National Post* entitled "The Country That Hates Itself."

Among other things, this is what she wrote:

> Multiculturalism has exacerbated the alienation that has left so many British Muslims vulnerable to the siren song of jihad. In addition, Britain has been unravelling its identity for decades, and multiculturalism has been the outcome. Since World War Two, Britain's elite has suffered from a collective collapse of cultural nerve. Many things contributed: postwar exhaustion, the collapse of the British Empire (and therefore the national purpose) and post-colonial flagellatory guilt of the kind that white western liberals have made their specialty.

> This left the British establishment vulnerable to the revolutionary ideology of the New Left, at the core of which lay a hatred of western society. As a consequence, the British elite decided not only that the British nation was an embarrassment, but also that the very idea of a nation was an anachronism. Britain had to be unravelled and a new world order constructed from principles unatainted by the particulars of national culture.

So schools no longer transmitted the British national story and the country's bedrock values. Immigrant children were taught instead that their culture was the community they came from, and children were left in ignorance of British history and taught that their values were whatever they wanted them to be.

A New Visible Minority

Hatred of Western Society? Unravelling of a nation? A new world order? Failure to teach our children their national experience? Any of this sound familiar?

The unravelling of Britain and the creation of a new world order is at this juncture only the speculation of a few. Here in Canada our unravelling and creation of a new order is guaranteed by figures and projections supplied by our own government. Perhaps not a new *world* order, but definitely a new Canadian order—a "New Canada"—where, in our large cities at least, those of European ancestry are becoming the new visible minority and the founding culture in English Canada is being replaced by a boatload of new cultures.

Frankly, I don't understand why there seems to be such reluctance to tackle the real problem. Surely everyone can see what is inevitable if we don't quickly change our policy.

If we continue importing non-Europeans at three or four times the rate of Europeans, then it's only a matter of time until a stranger getting off an airplane at Toronto's Pearson International Airport might be shocked to think he's made a mistake and landed in Bangkok, Mogadishu, New Delhi or Hong Kong—all wonderful places, to be sure—but they are not Canada!

Mark Steyn, in his controversial book *America Alone*, concerns himself almost exclusively with Islamic imperialism and advances a plethora of facts, figures and opinions to back him up, but he's missing the boat badly in Canada. In fact, what Steyn is unintentionally doing is dragging a red herring along the 401. The Yellowhead Highway as well!

The problem that confronts us here up north of 49 is not a burgeoning Muslim population. After all, Statistics Canada says Muslims will only comprise seven per cent of Canada's population by 2031. Muslim immigration poses its own special problems, but the real and very present danger here is the burgeoning population of immigrants from a multitude of non-European countries, most of which have very little appreciation, if any, of Western values.

In concentrating on the few thousand Muslims who arrive yearly and worrying only about them, we ignore the quarter million or so immigrants and refugees of other religions and cultures flocking to our major cities every year.

Muslims will not create "New Canada." The sheer numbers of immigrants from non-European nations, only some of whom are

Muslims, are already doing it. The tidal wave of newcomers with no understanding of the Canadian story will soon completely overwhelm us and create in the process hundreds of cultural and religious ghettos—none of which bear any resemblance to the Canada that you and I grew up in.

It is uncertain if such a nation can even continue to exist as a singular cohesive entity. If we have driven ourselves half-crazy trying to accommodate two languages and two cultures, imagine trying to govern a vast nation like ours with a couple of dozen Quebec-like city-states, each with vying interests that, since their inhabitants know nothing about Canada, cannot have the best interests of Canada at heart.

Not long ago, during a discussion on my program about immigration, an angry young man who identified himself as coming from Afghanistan called to take me to task. "What do you mean, many new Canadians can't have the best interests of Canada at heart?" he asked. He was mad as hell.

"How can you have the best interests of Canada at heart," I asked, "when you probably know absolutely nothing about this country, its history, its geography or the aspirations of its people?"

He tried to shout me down but I began to ask him some basic questions. "Who was Canada's first prime minister?" He had no idea. "Who's the prime minister today?" Another blank. "What is Queen's Park?" Silence. "How many provinces do we have?" More dead air.

My worst fears were realized. This young new Canadian knew absolutely nothing about Canada yet, in all probability, come the next election he will be voting for an MP to govern us.

I am not suggesting all recent immigrants are this ignorant of their new home, but once again let's throw political correctness to the wind and suggest that probably the majority doesn't know a whole lot more than my caller. Fact is, these days most newcomers to this country can't speak, read or write a word of English or French and, since they will most likely move into a large ghetto of similar ethnicity, will have no need to do so. They will nonetheless help to decide how the country—about which they know precious little—is to be run.

Let me give you another example of the growing danger we are plunging ourselves into.

Back in the days before the Harper government outlawed the Tamil Tigers in Canada, Tamil leaders boasted that since they were about 200,000 strong in Toronto and area they essentially controlled almost a dozen different ridings. This is probably an exaggeration, but even if it was only half true it's a scary thought and is surely one of the shoals that lies just off our port bow. Tamil votes were what Paul Martin was trolling for when he attended a Tamil Tiger fundraising event against the advice of CSIS in 2000.

Think of it. Who do you suppose most Tamils will vote for in a Federal election—the candidate who promises to do the best job for

Canada or the candidate who promises to do the best job for the Tamils? If the Harper Government had turned back the MV *Sun Sea* with its 492 Tamils, do you think there's a Tamil in Toronto who would ever vote Conservative? I could ask the same question of most other large, ghettoized ethnic communities and get the same answer. In these days of minority governments, it is entirely possible, indeed, quite probable, that a government can be elected on a foreign issue that has nothing to do with Canada.

Anyone with a British accent in London today will not hesitate to tell you that the number one problem facing the UK is immigration. Most Brits are worried sick they are losing their country to a multitude of foreigners, but during their most recent election you would have been hard-pressed to hear a single candidate even mention the matter. For a politician in England today to even raise what most consider is the number one problem would be the kiss of death. The reasons are simple: In an ever-growing number of constituencies, the immigrant vote is mandatory in order to win. And just to really finish you off, the left wing, politically correct, multicultural-propagating media will immediately label you as a prime bigot and not only destroy any chance of you winning, but your reputation as well, if you even suggest that immigration should be curbed.

We are not that far from a similar situation here in Canada.

Just for the heck of it, why don't we once again eschew political correctness and call a spade a spade? More than a few recent immigrants are doing one of two things. Either saving up their money in anticipation of returning to their native land with jangling pockets or sending large sums of money "back home." All perfectly legal, but hardly in the best interests of Canada. Money shipped out of Canada doesn't boost our economy!

In a major story in the *Vancouver Sun* in February 2008, several imams boasted that there were large numbers of Muslim men in the greater Toronto area with more than one wife. They went on to admit that it was not uncommon for some men to have four wives—all of whom are on welfare, along with their children. Often, I suspect, all living together in a few rooms.

While no reporter had the sense to ask the question, you can be almost certain that some of that welfare money is going back to Middle Eastern countries. I have taken phone calls from members of Ottawa's Somali community admitting that they are sending welfare money back to Somalia to help pay for relatives or friends to make their way to Canada as refugees. While they would never admit it, what they are talking about is sending enough money for their relatives or friends to buy the forged documents and return airfare required to get onto an airplane headed for the land of milk and honey and really, really easy welfare.

Once in the air, the documents required to get aboard the flight are either flushed down the toilet or more likely, handed back to an "agent" who probably has a handful of "clients" aboard the plane, all doing the same thing. Good environmentalists as they all are, the "agents" will recycle the documents, probably several times.

All of which makes you wonder why we are so careless with taxpayers' money in this country to allow a single cent of welfare money to be shipped out of Canada. Providing welfare to keep body and soul together is one thing. But money taken from taxpayers and then shipped to foreign lands? That's a whole different kettle of fish. There is no way to determine how much of this goes on, but you can be sure millions of welfare dollars are shipped out of Canada every year, very often to help cheat our system even more.

Now, project that forward to 2031 when, according to Stats Canada, visible minorities will comprise 63 per cent of Toronto's population and 60 per cent of Vancouver's population.

Jammed In
Where are they settling?

During the peak immigration years accompanying and immediately following the settlement of the Canadian West and again after WWII, not only were most immigrants arriving here from the UK, Europe and the US, most of them were spreading out across the land. They settled in places like Moncton, Quebec City, Ottawa, London, Winnipeg, Regina, Edmonton, and Calgary. They plowed the vast Prairies, dug for nickel in Sudbury and coal in Cape Breton, logged the Ottawa Valley, fished the Great Lakes and built cars in Windsor, and churches, schools and businesses from coast to coast. They forged cities, survived the Great Depression, fought with great distinction in two world wars and in the process created one of the finest nations on earth.

Most would have scoffed at the idea of jamming themselves into a few square miles of rabbit-like warrens. I doubt very much if governments of the day would have allowed it. Our ancestors came here to build

Canada, not an extension of the land from which they came.

Today, according to the latest census, more than 66 per cent of new immigrants and almost all refugees flock to Toronto, Vancouver and Montreal. Mostly Toronto and Vancouver.

In cold hard numbers that means close to 164,000 newcomers arrive every year in Toronto and Vancouver, placing tremendous stress on the infrastructure. The result is the kind of traffic congestion that drives most Torontonians mad, the city's garbage has to be trucked to Michigan, and crime rates continue to climb in both cities. In fact, the latest figures indicate that members of Toronto's black population are at greater risk of dying from gunshot wounds than blacks in New York City. Vancouver has what is generally accepted as the world's worst drug problem and the country's highest gun-crime rate. Both cities are experiencing skyrocketing welfare, education and health care costs.

About 46 cents of every tax dollar flowing into Ontario government coffers today is spent on health care. The Ontario government forecasts that as much as 70 cents of every tax dollar may have to go towards health care withing the next 12 years. While accurate figures are impossible to calculate, some health care experts say they believe as much as 25 per cent of Ontario's health costs are directly attributable to recent immigrants who are jamming our hospitals, doctors' offices and clinics. Today, the bulk of newcomers to Canada are from areas with very poor health care and, in some cases, from areas where diseases such as tuberculosis, which up until recently was almost wiped out in Canada, are common.

Every week dozens, sometimes hundreds, of pregnant women with dual citizenship arrive at Vancouver's airport from Hong Kong and Macau. In a few hours, days or weeks, they give birth to a brand new Canadian child and then head back to their permanent homes in China. There are times when Chinese women with Canadian citizenship occupy the majority of Vancouver's maternity wards.

It is estimated that as many as half a million Chinese from Hong Kong and Macau now have Canadian passports. Giving birth to your child in Canada accomplishes three things: first, you get first-rate health care, second, the care comes at Canada's expense, and third, your child automatically receives Canadian citizenship.

In his 2000 annual report to the Ontario Legislature, Gord Miller, Ontario's Environmental Commissioner, warned that any plan based on continuing population growth and consumption of resources is not sustainable. Even though "sustainable" is the catchphrase of the day, nobody paid any attention.

No one, it seems, has the courage to admit that one of the main reasons our health care costs are skyrocketing, while waiting lists grow longer, is that about 150,000 to 175,000 immigrants, many from Third World countries, arrive in Ontario every year, many requiring immediate health services. Add another 50,000 or 60,000 temporary workers and a slew of refugee claimants and, Ontario, we have a problem! If you don't believe me, show up at a hospital emergency ward in any of our major cities tomorrow!

The Money Pit

Unfortunately, there are no formal studies to give us anything more than an educated guess as to what adding three or four hundred thousand newcomers to Canada every year costs us, but Herb Grubel, Senior Fellow at the Fraser Institute and Professor of Economics (Emeritus) at Simon Fraser University, has come up with some figures that should scare the bejabbers out of everyone.

Grubel, writing in the book *The Effects of Mass Immigration on Canadian Living Standards and Society*, has done the math and concluded that just to accommodate the number of immigrants arriving annually in British Columbia, about 15,000 new dwelling units (apartments or houses) have to be built for them every year. That's 1,250 every month or about 280 every week if the immigrants are to enjoy the same housing standards as the rest of Canadians.

While he doesn't say it, this is undoubtedly the main reason that the cost of housing continues to skyrocket in both Toronto and

Vancouver, where most immigrants immediately settle. If they need 280 new housing units every week in Vancouver, can you just imagine how many must be built in Toronto, which accepts three of four times as many immigrants?

But it doesn't end there.

Grubel points out that if only half of the immigrant families in Vancouver own one car, 5,000 new cars are added to the region's traffic every year. It's no wonder, he says, that improvements to the highway and public transit systems cannot keep up with the demand. "The increased traffic, often slowed in jams, results in more air pollution."

At this point, I can't help but note that for the most part those "progressive" thinkers who always oppose so-called urban sprawl and the construction of high-rise buildings in the downtown areas of our cities and who also moan about auto emissions causing global warming are the same "progressives" who are busy encouraging mass immigration. Just where our friends on the left think we are supposed to accommodate more than a quarter of a million newcomers every year is unclear. Certainly not in their backyards!

Grubel then goes on to point out that if every family of three immigrants in Vancouver has one child attending school, 10,000 new places have to be created in educational institutions every year and many new teachers have to be employed. He also talks about the increased demand for medical care, hospital beds, social assistance, fire and police protection, water supplies, sewers, and so on.

97

Then he makes a very interesting observation. Let me quote him:

> In a fundamental sense, the inadequacy of infrastructure facilities and the persistence of pollution and crowding are not due to population growth and immigration but to the inadequate rate of construction needed to prevent them. This statement is correct as far as it goes. It neglects the fact that the existing methods for planning and building the infrastructure always lag behind the need for them. It would indeed be highly desirable if these methods could be changed, perhaps through the greater involvement of the private sector and the streamlining of the political approval process, the granting of building permits, and the securing of financial resources. The problem is that efforts to speed up infrastructure projects have a long history and have had very little success. If anything, the growth in the public's environmental concern in recent decades has increased the lag between the creation and elimination of the inadequacy of Canada's infrastructure. Until this lag has been eliminated, it follows that immigration, which is determined by deliberate policies of the federal government, aggravates these inadequacies and imposes costs on Canadians.

And here's a shocker: In another study conducted by Grubel, it was determined that in the year 2000 various government services consumed by each immigrant who arrived ten years earlier in 1990 amounted to a net total of $6,294.

Roughly translated, it means that even after ten years of living in Canada, on average, each immigrant is costing us taxpayers about $6,000 more per year than the immigrant contributes in taxes or services.

And even more shocking, according to Grubel, in the year 2002 there were 2.9 million immigrants who had arrived during the preceding 12 years. At the rate of roughly $6,000 per immigrant per year, it means that in just one year—2002—the net cost to taxpayers for all immigrants who had arrived between 1990 and 2002 was about $18 billion—16 per cent of Canada's total budget and more than the Federal government spent on health care!

And, as Grubel points out, this is money that will never be recovered even if, eventually, the income of immigrants reaches the same level as those born in this country.

For those of you interested in pursuing this matter of the economics of immigration in much more detail, let me recommend that you contact the Fraser Institute. It publishes by far the best research on the entire question of mass immigration in a book I have already referred to entitled *The Effects of Mass Immigration on Canadian Living Standards and Society*.

Out Of Control

It is also in the book *The Effects of Mass Immigration on Canadian Living Standards and Society* that James Bisset writes:

> Another issue that is seldom discussed is that most of the newcomers are coming from Asian countries and consequently are transforming the demographic content of our major urban areas. It seems likely that

if immigration intake continues at the present level these two cities in Canada [Toronto and Vancouver] will over time become predominately Asian.... This may or may not be desirable but surely it is something that should be discussed openly and done so without accusations of racism. In other words, there are important implications involved when the traditional demographic and cultural nature of a city or country is subject to sudden change. If our immigration policy is designed to encourage more diversity and to promote multiculturalism, then we should be told that this is one of its objectives. What guarantee do we have that diversity in itself is a desirable objective? At what point does diversity mutate into a form of colonization?

Bissett goes on to say:

Many of the reasons with which Canada justifies its high immigration intake are simply not valid and the economic and social costs are not open to discussion or debate. The policy is out of control and desperately in need of reform. We may not have reached the tipping point but, if we continue to sleepwalk into the twenty-first century and ignore this issue, we may find out too late that Canada has been unalterably changed without either the consent of its people or a full awareness on their part of what is happening.

Colonization?

To be perfectly honest the idea that our major cities are being colonized never entered my mind until I contemplated Bissett's question: "At what point does diversity mutate into a form of colonization?"

Let me ask you: When Asian or other immigrants comprise the majority of the population in places like Toronto and Vancouver, is that not in fact a form of colonization? Especially when you consider that, rather than dispersing throughout the general population and gradually integrating into the Canadian mainstream, what we are seeing are ever-larger ethnic ghettos within our major cities.

And what about that great catchphrase so favoured by the "left"— racial diversity? How much diversity is there likely to be in a city whose population is 60 or 70 per cent Asian? How diverse can a community be if the population is 70 per cent Dutch, or Spanish, or

Muslim or Hindu? Why the assumption that a population comprised of 70 per cent Europeans requires more diversity, but 70 or 80 per cent Asian is very desirable?

And if the Asian or the Dutch or the Hindu population continues to grow at a rate four times faster than any other, how long will it be until the 70 per cent majority becomes 75 or 80 per cent? Let's be frank here, if heritage Canadians are not producing enough babies to compensate for those who die, how long will it be until those of European ancestry are reduced to a tiny, insignificant minority?

All of this may be a wonderful thing, but is this really what we want to happen here? Are we really prepared to become a series of colonies for the citizens of repressive, sometimes dangerous and often failed, states?

Shouldn't we at the very least be free to openly discuss it without being branded racist or worse?

Actually, when you examine the demographics, you are compelled to wonder if the word colonization is really applicable. Because, in fact, some of our ethnic communities are a kind of de facto extension of the countries from which their inhabitants came.

During the great waves of immigration that settled this country and up until the early 1990s, newcomers understood only too well that once they boarded the ship and headed west for Canada's shores, it was a permanent goodbye to their country of birth.

In order to survive in their new home they knew they would have to quickly adapt to a new language, new customs, new work habits, a different climate, even a different way of shopping and commuting. Many rules, laws and regulations would be different. Driving habits had to be adjusted and while they probably didn't think about it too much, they had to adapt to new forms of entertainment and learn about new cultural icons and heroes. Heck, many even learned what an offside was in hockey!

In short, in order to thrive, or even survive, you had to become part of the warp and weft of the Canadian fabric, learning how to do things in the Canadian way.

There were very few, if any, welfare cheques for those who built this country. As my grandfather used to say, it was pretty much "root hog or die!"

The immigrant experience today is totally different. Different in obvious ways—plenty of welfare cheques, free health care for your entire family, free housing, free legal assistance, and a human rights commission to pretty well bankrupt anyone whom you claim offends you in any way. But the great danger to the well-being of this country may lie in some of the less obvious changes to what is now available to immigrants.

Satellite Danger

During the 2006 war between Israel and Hezbollah, I was shocked as I fielded call after call on my show from those making outrageous claims about Jewish atrocities being perpetrated against Palestinians. Many callers claimed they vehemently supported Hezbollah and would gladly fight for them.

They made incredible accusations that as many as three million Lebanese had been killed—that blackened bodies proved Israel was using chemical weapons and deliberately targeting children. The tired old fairytale about the Jews and George Bush engineering the attack on the twin towers was dragged out again and again. Several claimed they had seen pictures of Israeli soldiers sawing children's heads off and pouring acid into their eyes.

It was all so warped and fantastic I began to doubt we lived on the same planet or, at the very least, the same country! And in a way we did not.

Physically, the callers and I were in the same country, the same city for that matter. But psychologically we were literally continents apart. The callers had dragged their birth countries with them, in a matter of speaking. While their bodies were here in Canada, their hearts and minds were back in the villages, towns and cities they had not really left behind.

A Canadian friend of Lebanese descent explained it all to me.

"It's the satellites," he told me. Then he explained: "They're getting all their information, all their opinions, all their so-called facts directly from the 'old country.' It's all beamed directly into their living rooms from Arab television stations via satellite. It comes directly from the LBC [Lebanese Broadcasting Corporation] and that's the most balanced coverage of all. The really vicious stuff," he assured me, "the real hateful propaganda is coming from Al Jazeera, Egyptian TV, Syrian TV and worst of all, it's coming from Al-Manara."

Al-Manara, I learned, is Hezbollah's own private television network, directed at millions of Arabs around the world. Here in Canada, even though Hezbollah has been outlawed as a terrorist organization, its television station is viewed widely throughout the country. You can imagine the kind of bias it portrays at any given time, let alone during a war with Israel!

But it is not just Canada's Arab population that receives almost all of its information and entertainment from a distant land. The same holds true of virtually every ethnic community today.

Gone are the days when an immigrant arriving here from Italy or Spain had no choice but to learn the language in order to find out what was going on and also to be entertained. They tuned into "The Happy Gang" on CBC radio and a bit later they kept up with the stories of the day on "Front Page Challenge," or tapped their toes to "Don Messer's Jubilee." Their news and views were almost entirely from the Canadian perspective. They had no choice. Once in a while they might get a letter from "home," but essentially they were forced into a crash course on Canada and the "West."

The only really successful method of learning a new language is through total immersion. And that's exactly what immigrants up until recently experienced—total immersion in the Canadian experience.

They read Canadian newspapers, listened to Canadian radio, watched Canadian or American television, were forced to speak English or French on the job, on the bus, in restaurants and at their son's soccer game and before they knew it—lo and behold—they were Canadian. More proudly Canadian, in many cases, than people born here. There was no question about their children's nationality. No Italian-Canadian or Polish-Canadian or Hungarian-Canadian hyphens for them.

By the time their children were in Grade 4, they had probably adopted a favourite radio station, knew every song on the hit parade, and the girls went nuts over Paul Anka and the Beatles and the boys knew every hockey player in the NHL from watching "Hockey Night in Canada."

Little Shanghai

What a difference today! The owner of one of Toronto's largest Chinese restaurants explained it best not long ago when, in obvious exasperation, he told me about a recent visit he paid to Vancouver.

"There," he said, "restaurant owners were boasting how easy it is to get new workers. Just phone a guy in Hong Kong or Shanghai, tell him how many you need, and a week later you pick them up at the airport. They may come in as temporary workers but, the fact is, with the laws the way they are in Canada they can essentially stay as long as they wish. Sometimes forever.

"Convincing them to come is easy; just tell them it's just like home here in Vancouver. No difference. Leave big Shanghai and come to little Shanghai. You don't have to speak English; nobody here speaks English. You don't even have to give up your favourite TV program, because many of the Chinese channels are available here and you can get your hometown newspaper every day on the Internet. You bring your home with you to Canada, but the pay is a lot better."

I found his sentiments a little strange. "But you're Chinese," I said, "why does the fact some think Vancouver is just a little Shanghai bother you?"

He snapped back a reply. "No, I am not Chinese, I am Canadian. My wife is Canadian, my children are Canadian. I left China a long time ago to come to Canada not to little Shanghai. If I want to live in

China then I will fly over top of Vancouver and go back to China!"
God bless him, but how many recent immigrants do you suppose
feel the same way?

Believe me, when Italians came to Canada after the Second World
War they didn't come to little Rome. When Hungarians flocked here
after their revolution (1956/57) they didn't come to little Budapest
and when the Vietnamese Boat People made their way to our shores
(1979/80) they didn't find any little Saigon! No hometown TV or
radio. No familiar newspapers and magazines. It was: Get a job, learn
the language, adapt, adopt and adapt some more. Fast!

It was good for Canada, and you know something? Ask any of those
who came to Canada up until recently and almost without exception they will tell you converting to Canadianism fast was the best
thing that ever happened to them. Don't believe me? Ask anyone
who came here prior to the mid-1990s. Almost all will understand
and agree absolutely with that Toronto restaurant owner's sentiments. Canada has been very good for them and they have been very
good for Canada.

Homegrown Terrorism

The most worrisome terrorist trend in Canada is the increase in second- and third-generation Canadians who have become so "appallingly disenchanted" with life here they are contemplating or engaging in violence at home or abroad, the country's top spy says.

Richard Fadden, Director of the Canadian Security Intelligence Service [CSIS], highlighted the agency's concerns about radicalization of such domestic groups Tuesday during an appearance before a parliamentary committee. Such recruits to terrorism are relatively integrated into Canada, but for whatever reason, they develop connections to their former homelands and reject the essence of Canadian values, he said.

He said the agency is tracking more than 200 individuals in Canada with possible links to as many as 50 terrorist groups.

Speaking later to reporters, he said a number of people—approximately two dozen or more—have left Canada to engage in "violent jihad" and most have ended up heading overseas to get trained in

Afghanistan, Pakistan, Yemen or Somalia.

(Norma Greenaway, "CSIS boss flags homegrown terrorist trend,"
Canwest News Service, May 12, 2010)

. . .

It was also Fadden, of course, who created a great stir in the country
when he claimed that some "Ministers of the Crown" (provincial)
and municipal politicians had fallen under the influence of foreign
governments, something that surely should surprise no one.

. . .

One of the ringleaders of the so-called Toronto 18 has pleaded guilty
in mid-trial after a jury heard weeks of evidence that Fahim Ahmad
led a terror cell plotting to attack Parliament and nuclear targets.

Mr. Ahmad, 25, was being tried along with Steven Chand and Asad
Ansari on terrorism charges. It is the last of the trials associated with a
group of 18 men and youths arrested in the summer of 2006.

The jury heard earlier in the trial that Mr. Ahmad was the leader of a
terror cell and held two training camps to assess his recruits' suitabil-
ity to help him attack Parliament, electrical grids and nuclear stations.

[In one of the recorded videotapes recorded by police] ...Mr. Ahmad
can be heard suggesting going to Parliament Hill to "cut off some
heads" and "kill everybody."

("Guilty plea mid-trial from member of 'Toronto 18,'" The Globe and
Mail, *May 10, 2010)*

• • •

The first person charged under Canada's post-Sept. 11 law against raising funds for terrorist groups pleaded guilty in a Vancouver courtroom Tuesday morning.

Prapaharan Thambithurai of Maple, Ont., admitted raising money from Tamil immigrants in the Vancouver area, knowing that some of the money would end up funding the banned Tamil Tigers. He told them [donors] he was raising the money for humanitarian purposes, but later admitted to RCMP investigators he knew the Sri Lankan rebel group would inevitably keep as much as half of the money.

(Jane Wolsak, "Tamil Tiger fundraiser pleads guilty," The Canadian Press, May 11, 2010)

• • •

Twenty-five years ago this month, Sikh-Canadian terrorists blew up Air India Flight 182, killing 329 people. To this day, it stands as the greatest act of terrrorism in this nation's history. It would be nice to report that Sikh radicalism is a thing of the past in Canada. But it is not. Even as Sikhs living in India have rejected militancy in recent years, many Canadian Sikhs still are active in the campaign to create an independent nation called Khalistan. At Canadian Sikh parades and gurdwaras, controversies still erupt over the inclusion of separatist groups, as well as posters and photographs that honour the "martyrs" who murdered Indian politicians and military leaders.

("Tread carefully on Sikh history," National Post, June 2, 2010)

• • •

One outspoken critic of Canada's immigration and refugee policies is David Harris, former Chief of Strategic Planning for CSIS and now Director of the International and Terrorist Intelligence program at INSIGNIS Strategic Research Inc. in Ottawa.

In an interview with me not long ago he described Canada's immigration and refugee program as a "death wish." We cannot possibly screen more than a quarter of a million new Canadians every year, plus another 35,000 to 40,000 refugees. "Furthermore," he said, "we cannot properly integrate them into Canadian society.

"Another problem," he went on, "is that while most people who come here from other lands want nothing more than to settle into a peaceful life, we allow radicals to infiltrate the ethnic communities. Radicals who intimidate recent arrivals into giving money for terrorist causes, often threatening family members who remain behind."

This fact was never more evident than in the Tamil community of Toronto where, prior to the defeat of the Tamil Tigers, tens of thousands of dollars were being extorted from local Tamil families every year.

Threats of torture and death for family members still in Sri Lanka were commonplace. Hasaka Rathnamalala of the Sri Lankan United Association of Canada called it "homegrown terrorism," stated Lesley Ciarula Taylor in an article entitled "Group slams Tigers' Toronto 'terrorism' in the *Toronto Star* on February 4, 2009.

Even after the Harper government banned the Tamil Tigers in

Canada, Rathnamalala said the intimidation and extortion continued in Toronto where the tactics included "...smashing car windshields, looting homes, computerized identity theft and threats of closing down businesses."

The homegrown terrorism doesn't just stalk the Tamils. It is obvious a bitter and often violent battle is being waged coast-to-coast within Sikh communities, pitting those who support a separate Sikh state in India against those who just want to get on with their lives. Canada's worst terrorist attack, the Air India murders, is just one manifestation of the extent to which some Sikh separatists are prepared to go. The battle is heating up with Sikh blood flowing freely. Control of the temples means control of considerable wealth that can be funnelled into the separatist cause. Very clearly this is one more area where age-old hatreds have not been left behind, but dragged across an ocean and planted in our soil.

When Sikh extremists blew up Air India Flight 182, 329 innocent people died, but they are not the only victims of this terrible feud, which Ujjal Dosanjh says is growing more dangerous. Dosanjh himself was savagely beaten in Vancouver in 1985 after speaking out against religious violence. But perhaps the most chilling story of all is that involving Tara Singh Hayer, publisher of North America's largest Punjabi-language newspaper. The sheer cowardice of his murder takes your breath away.

In August of 1988, Hayer, who had begun writing editorials condemning violence within the Sikh separatist movement, was gunned down in his office by masked men who left him for dead. Hayer survived, but was partially paralyzed and confined for the rest of his life to a wheelchair.

Move the calendar ahead about ten years. Dusk is just settling over the West Coast on November 18, 1998, when Hayer, tired from a day at his desk at the *Indo-Canadian Times*, pulls his car into the garage of his comfortable home in suburban Surrey. As he struggles to move his crippled body from his car seat into a wheelchair, a masked man steps out of the gloom, holds a gun to Hayer's head, and fires.

Twelve years later, not a single arrest has been made. Police say many people must know who the killer is, but are too afraid to come forward.

In addition to criticizing the Sikh extremism, Hayer was the last remaining witness for the prosecution in the Air India case. The only other witness was murdered earlier.

Some Cultures are Just Plain Awful

In an interview published in the June 2006 edition of *Macleans* magazine, David Harris said, "One of the things is to deal with our nearly out-of-control immigration and refugee situation. To the extent we're bringing in some people from some regions where liberal, pluralist, democratic, live-and-let-live, Charter-type values are considered anathema, are even considered devilish—we need to be sure that we have the capacity to absorb people properly. It's important to emphasize that absorption includes the absorption of our broader values of tolerance, civility and so on."

While Harris doesn't come right out and say it, what he is doubtless alluding to is the fact that some races and cultures seem better able to adapt to Canadian values and laws than others.

No doubt there will be protests over any discussion of this issue, but we've got to be honest and once again be damned with political correctness.

There can be little doubt that it is more difficult for people from some countries to, as Harris says, absorb "Canada's broader values of tolerance, civility and so on." And with rare exception that holds true regardless of the education, skill or personality of the immigrant.

If you come from a country with little, if any, experience with democracy and all that entails, you will likely have difficulty understanding and subscribing to things like freedom of speech and the responsibilities of those living in a free society. If you come from a police state, your view of law and order and those who administer it will likely be different from those raised in a law-abiding, free society. If you come from a culture where women are devalued, you may find it more difficult than others to deal with a female boss, police officer or teacher.

It is not racism to discuss this, it is simply common sense to acknowledge this fact. We see it all around us.

As just one example of the manner in which some immigrant populations have great difficulty integrating into Canadian society is a story featured in the April 17, 2010, edition of the *Ottawa Citizen* headlined "Gangs Targeting Visible Minorities."

The story quotes Ottawa Police Chief Vern White as warning us that gangs are recruiting visible-minority youths into the drug trade and social workers are worried the situation will become much worse if the ethnic communities don't take the problem seriously.

White notes that close to two dozen Somali youths have been murdered in Alberta during the past few years, some having moved from the Ottawa area.

Farah Aw-Osman, a long-time social worker in Ottawa, claims he's not surprised but what really worries him is that "very few people in either the Somali or Muslim communities are taking this seriously." He also noted that "… ethnic and faith-based communities are often completely unprepared to deal with issues such as drug dependency."

But it is Mohamed Sofa, a Somali youth worker, who puts his finger on the real problem when he asks this question: The Somali community has been in Ottawa for close to two decades, so why are so many of its members still living in low-income housing and struggling with crime and poverty issues?

He points to a recent study by the Social Planning Council of Ottawa that shows that in 2006, fully 61 per cent of Ottawa Somalis still live in poverty and 64 per cent of that community is under the age of 24.

Very clearly if more than 60 per cent of a particular ethnic community still lives in poverty after nearly 20 years in this country, this country has a serious problem!

But why would we be surprised? Let's use common sense here. If those from countries where law and order, democracy, women's rights and freedom of speech are anathema are distributed across the country, spread across several thousand miles, there are likely to be far fewer problems of integration than if we jam thousands of people who share these sentiments into ghettos. Because in those ghettos, their cultural norms, attitudes and lifestyle will likely be supported and reinforced not only by technology but also by everyone around them.

I suspect that had we settled a few Somali families in each of several dozen communities that value hard work, education and adherence to the law, we would have far fewer problems. And so would they.

I suspect the same holds true with the Tamil population of Toronto. If we didn't have about 200,000 of them jammed into a few square miles surely they would be much safer from "homegrown terrorism."

If Sikhs were not packed into Surrey and Brampton, life for them and for us would likely be much more serene.

Campus Chaos

There was a time when coal miners took a canary with them down into the depths. The theory was that if the canary keeled over it was a sign they had all better make a run for cleaner air and a safer place. Let me tell you, if canaries were predictors of trouble just ahead in our country, there would be a lot of dead canaries on our university campuses!

Racial and ethnic tensions, strife, name-calling, harassment, even violence have broken out on several Canadian campuses in recent years, and it continues.

In February of 2009, mostly Jewish students had to be rescued by police when pro-Palestinian students chased them into a York University campus building, threatened them and refused to allow them to leave. It was not an isolated incident.

Two days of violent street protests in Montreal forced the cancellation of an address former Israeli Prime Minister Benjamin Netanyahu was scheduled to make at Concordia University in September 2002.

Israel Apartheid Week, marked at many Canadians universities, including Carleton Univerity and the University of Ottawa, is very clearly a deliberate escalation of the discord that exists between Arabs and Jews on too many campuses.

Things are so tense that only two days after the violent protests forced the cancellation of the Netanyahu address, conflict flared again at Concordia—this time, believe it or not, over food.

According to Ingrid Peritz and Tu Thanh Ha, writing in *The Globe and Mail* on September 14, 2002, "…student clubs at Concordia put out their colourful tables for orientation week. One table was operated by a Palestinian student group offering key chains and pamphlets that were critical of Israel. At another were students from the Jewish group Hillel, who were offering falafel and other items.

Suddenly, a representative from the Palestinian table stepped up to the Hillel table. He accused the Jewish group of cultural theft for selling falafel.

"Hillel is stealing Arab food," he shouted in the crowded hall.

The *Globe* story goes on to say, "The fact that a snack food could become a symbol of cultural imperialism says a lot about the state of Jewish-Arab relations at Concordia…. For years, Concordia has been turned into mini-Middle East, divided by the upheavals tearing at Israel and the Arab world."

Other Concordia University incidents provide some graphic examples of what some describe as a state of semi-siege.

Palestinian students created a mock graveyard in the main building with elaborate headstones made of plastic foam. Each of the 44 graves was marked with the name and photo of a Palestinian killed by Israeli forces. On the way out of the exhibit students had to go through a checkpoint where they were made to produce identification and were inspected with a mock metal detector.

In 2001, the Concordia student union produced a handbook that praised the intifada and urged the burning of the Canadian flag.

Arab students protested a poster for a lecture by a Hillel speaker in which there was a reference to "Palestinian terrorism." They had to change the wording. Arab students created a poster for one of their lectures that featured an Israeli bulldozer atop a pile of corpses—it was not changed.

The worst event was, of course, the protests against the Netanyahu speech.

Here's how *The Globe and Mail* (September 14, 2002) described what happened:

> As the day of the speech dawned, 150 security officers from the Montreal police force, the RCMP and the university began to mass around Concordia. Riot police lined up in full gear in the street, while other officers stood watch from rooftops around the Hall Building where the former prime minister was to speak.
>
> At first the protests were spirited but contained, with pro-Palestinian demonstrators waving flags and shouting anti-Israel slogans. But emotions flared. Security began to break down.
>
> As people tried to enter the building for the speech, protesters, encouraged by organizers on megaphones, resisted and blocked the way. A Montreal rabbi's skullcap was ripped from his head. Thomas Hecht, a Holocaust survivor who heads the Canada-Israel Committee's Quebec branch, was pushed against a wall, spat on and reportedly kicked in the groin.

The *Globe* story continues, saying that there was a claim by some Palestinians that some Jewish students groped some of the Arab's women chests, but others have denied this.

In the tumult, protesters managed to enter the building through Java U, a campus café. They swarmed the escalators leading to the lobby were Mr. Netanyahu was to speak. The protest spun so far out of control that the speech finally had to be cancelled.

The violence actually continued for two days and at one point spread to nearby buildings where windows were broken and other students assaulted.

According to the *Globe*, "Fed in part by recent waves of immigrants and refugees from Arab countries, Concordia is now home to an estimated 5,000 Muslim students, one-fifth of the student body. Another 1,500 to 2,000 students are Jewish."

Very clearly, our immigration and multicultural policies aren't working very well at Concordia or York, or at many other universities, for that matter.

When the most privileged and pampered among us, our university students—the leaders of tomorrow—start fighting over snack foods it's time some alarm bells began to ring someplace! Especially when you consider that Canada has provided a safe refuge for many of these students who fled the conditions they are now seeking to create in this country.

What do you think? I've asked this before. I ask it again. Does any of this make sense to you?

Women's Rights In Some
of the Cultures We Are Importing

A veteran Iranian human rights activist warns that Sakineh Moham-madie Ashtiani, a mother of two, could be stoned to death at any moment under the terms of a death sentence handed down by Iranian authorities.

Only an international campaign designed to pressure the regime in Tehran can save her life, according to Mina Ahadi, head of the International Committee Against Stoning and the Death Penalty.

"Legally, it's all over," Ahadi said Sunday. "It's a done deal. Sakineh can be stoned at any minute. That is why we have decided to start a very broad, international public movement. Only that can help."

Ashtiani, 42, will be buried up to her chest, according to an Amnesty International report citing the Iranian penal code. The stones that will be hurled at her will be large enough to cause pain but not so large as to kill her immediately.

Ashtiani, who is from the northern city of Tabriz, was convicted of adultery in 2006. She was forced to confess after being subjected to 99 lashes, human rights lawyer Mohammad Mostafaei said Thursday in a telephone interview from Tehran.

She later retracted that confession and has denied any wrongdoing. Her conviction was based not on evidence but on the determination of three out of five judges, Mostafaei said. She has asked forgiveness from the court but the judges refused to grant clemency.

The circumstances of Ashtiani's case make it not an exception but the rule in Iran. The majority of those sentenced to death by stoning are women....

Article 74 of the Iranian penal code requires at least four witnesses—four men or three men and two women—for an adulterer to receive a stoning sentence....

But there were no witnesses in Ashtiani's case. Often, said Ahadi, husbands turn wives in to get out of a marriage.

(*"Human rights activist tries to stop death by stoning for Iranian woman," CNN Wire Staff, July 5, 2010*)

Editor's note: The Iranian government, under worldwide pressure, has relented and agreed that for the time being they will not put Ms. Ashtiani to death. But, as this book goes to press, her death sentence is still in force.

. . .

The following article by Aruna Papp appeared in the *National Post*, August 14, 2009:

> Given the media commentary in recent years about certain high-profile alleged "honour killings" in this country, Canadians might have the impression that such hideous crimes are confined to the Muslim community. That is not the case. Unchallenged violence against women, including honour killing, is also a distressing feature of Sikh, Hindu and South Asian Christian communities.
>
> I know. I am ethnically Indian, raised as a Christian. I arrived in Canada at the age of 21, married, with two little girls of my own. In my father's house, I was the eldest of six daughters. From an early age, I, like millions of other females, knew that girls were dispensable. We suffered from what *Post* columnist Barbara Kay has called "ideological terrorism," a brutal brainwashing technique that internalizes the idea in both men and women that women are unworthy creatures.
>
> My grandmother's and mother's complicity in perpetuating the myth of family honour was typical of the honour/shame culture. Victims themselves—my mother was abused by her in-laws—they reflexively punished their daughters for what they had been taught was the misfortune of being female.
>
> My father's mother, for example, never missed an opportunity to voice her disapproval of the females born to her beloved son. Pointing at her granddaughters, she would say for all to hear, "Look at those ugly creatures, eating my son out of home and house. What choice do I have but to drop them in the well one by one?"

Sympathetic neighbours would nod understandingly. Our indoctrinated mother often dealt with her helplessness by thrashing us, she and father begging us to plead with God to give us a brother.

Traumatizing reminders of female worthlessness were everywhere. Once, fetching milk for the family morning tea, I saw a baby girl thrown by the roadside with her umbilical cord attached.

I was 11 when I witnessed 19-year-old Kiran set ablaze by her two brothers because she had a boyfriend and had "dishonoured" her family. No one tried to save her. Everyone just stood and watched. Later, the neighbours danced at one of the brother's wedding celebrations. The terror is continual and all-consuming. Women and young girls quickly learn that the smallest deviations from purity, such as lifting your eyelashes and looking up at the wrong time at the wrong person, can have horrible results—as they did for Kiran.

Eventually, one starts to believe that family honour and the necessity for self-sacrifice to avoid family shame is normal. The brainwashing begins at birth and is reinforced through music on the radio, cinema, stories, legends, folktales and neighbourhood gossip. It begins in the old country but it does not remain there.

Once in Canada some of us dare to think we can reach out and grab a little bit of self worth—we dare to feel loved or wanted. After all, we now live in a culture where female empowerment is the theoretical norm: Women's worth is all around us, in music, movies, magazines, books, even self-esteem-building classes.

But in many cases this culture of freedom is no match for the culture of origin. I know many women who tried to disengage from the past.

They were sent back to the old country to be married off to men they had never met. In my own case, the older man my father forced me to marry in India abused me for many years before I finally divorced him and got on with my true Canadian life of equality and autonomy.

Others who rebel are not as lucky. Some are killed in the name of honour. It only has to happen to one girl or woman. The rest get the picture and fall into line. Some even start to sermonize themselves. The threat is renewed. The reality is reaffirmed.

For the past 27 years, I have been working with these fellow victims of culturally approved violence: women who have been threatened, beaten, strangled, locked away in dark basements, taken to the old country and abandoned or married off to strangers in the name of family honour, family shame and saving face.

A report by the United Nations Population Fund states that "at least 60 million girls" who should be alive are "missing from various populations, mostly in Asia. "The acceptance of the scapegoating of women is a problem for the honour/shame societies themselves. The failure to acknowledge the plight and come to the rescue of the victims among us is a problem for all Canadians.

—Aruna Papp

Papp is a therapist/counsellour at Family Services, York Region, in Toronto. She is the author of a recent report entitled *Culturally Driven Violence Against Women: A Growing Problem in Canada's Immigration Communities*, in which she is highly critical of South Asian communities in Canada and what she describes as "political correctness amongst influential Canadians who, in order not to racialize honour killings, describe them as domestic violence, which is a different social and cultural phenomenon from an honour killing."

On July 12, 2010, Papp, on behalf of the Frontier Centre for Public Policy, released a list of 14 recommendations she says would help to address the issue of violence against women in various ethnic communities.

Among those recommendations was a plea to the federal government to require prospective female immigrants to attend training sessions in their home country to learn about their rights and Canadian culture and values, stressing gender equality. Also recommended are mandatory orientation sessions for male sponsors. These sessions, she says, should stress Canadian values and sponsorship laws with particular attention paid to gender equality.

Another important recommendation from Papp and the Centre is that prospective male sponsors should be investigated to check how many times they have been married and their pattern of sponsorship. It should be documented as to how the previous spouse is being financially supported and, as a further recommendation, men should be checked for any criminal record in Canada and their country of origin with an eye to any complaints of spousal abuse.

One recommendation I find especially interesting, and no doubt very worthwhile, is that there needs to be government-funded programs on local and national television and radio in various languages that educate women on gender equality and that remind abusers that there will be consequences for abusing women.

The final recommendation is that leaders in South Asian communities must be pressured to speak out frequently and sincerely against the practice of abusing girls and women.

Rona Ambrose, Minister for the Status of Women, condemned honour killings and called on all women's groups and local communities to work together with the government to combat "heinous abuses of power" at a news conference held in Toronto on July 12, 2010.

When you stop and think about it, if a man arrives here, let's say, from Saudi Arabia, where women have very few rights, and he watches only Saudi television, reads only Saudi publications and settles in a Saudi neighbourhood, it is quite possible he doesn't even know that we treat women as equals in Canada. How would he learn this? Very little in the immigration process instructs him about women's rights. Nothing he sees or hears on Saudi TV is going to clue him in. Ditto Saudi publications. As for the Saudis in his neighbourhood, they probably believe that they've only moved to a considerably colder Riyadh and see no reason to change the way they live or think.

Our multiculturalism policies, after all, insist that the Saudi culture is the equal of Canada's and tells the Saudis exactly that.

I'm using Saudi Arabia as just one example of what we are dealing with and how immigration has changed so radically from just a few years ago. Once again, we've got to scrap political correctness and state facts.

One of the most serious issues we have to address is that many of the countries now providing us with immigrants do not value girls and women as highly as they value boys and men.

Ask any female teacher in a classroom filled with boys from Middle Eastern countries how difficult this often makes their job. It is just not part of the culture of many countries to show the same respect to women as to men, and trouble is inevitable.

"You try disciplining an eight-year-old boy who, at home, is able to order his older sisters and probably even his mother around," one frustrated female teacher told me the other day. "Some of these young boys come into my classroom like little potentates and God help any woman who tries to get them straightened around to our way of thinking!"

Sorry to state the truth, but along with most Middle Eastern countries, this devaluation of women also applies to China and India.

Is Gendercide Coming Here?

The Chinese Academy of Social Sciences has recently warned that within ten years 24 million Chinese men will find themselves condemned to permanent bachelorhood. "Among Chinese men aged 19 and younger the prospects of finding a bride are even worse. By 2020," states the Academy, "there will be 30 million to 40 million more males in this age group than females."

In China they are called *guanggun* or "bare branches"—young males with little prospect of marriage.

According to the highly regarded weekly newsmagazine *The Economist*, in many parts of China the ratio of boys to girls is now 124 to 100. In a cover story published the first week of March 2010, *The Economist* went on to say "…these ratios [boys to girls] are biologically impossible without human intervention."

The Economist is obviously referring to China's one-baby policy introduced by the government in 1979 to control spiralling population growth. Couples are penalized by wage cuts and reduced access to social services if they have more than one child and since girls are not valued as highly as boys, it has resulted in a very high number of female fetuses being aborted and, according to some reports in some parts of China, the killing of newborn baby girls is quite common.

The international organization Gendercide Watch states:

> The phenomenon of female infanticide is as old as many cultures, and has likely accounted for millions of gender-selective deaths throughout history. It remains a critical concern in a number of Third World countries today, notably the two most populous countries on earth, China and India. In all cases, specifically female infanticide reflects the low status accorded to women in many parts of the world; it is arguably the most brutal and destructive manifestation of the anti-female bias that pervades "patriarchal" societies. It is closely linked to the phenomena of sex-selective abortion which targets female fetuses almost exclusively, and neglect of girl children.

Not Just China

According to an article published in the *Boston Globe*, March 14, 2010, written by *Globe* columnist Jeff Jacoby:

> In India each year, it is estimated that as many as a million baby girls are aborted by parents determined not to raise a daughter.
>
> Those unborn girls are the victims of a fierce cultural preference for

boys—and of modern imaging technology that makes it easy to learn the sex of a baby in the womb. Ultrasound scans started becoming widely available in India in the 1980s; since then, an estimated ten million female babies have been destroyed during pregnancy.

Sex-selection tests are illegal in India. So are sex-selective abortions. But the laws are rarely enforced and easily circumvented. Rather than openly disclose the sex of a fetus after an ultrasound exam, for example, some Indian doctors signal the results by giving the parents pink or blue candies or candles. Others dispense with subtlety altogether, advertising their services with such brazen slogans as "Spend 500 rupees now and save 50,000 rupees later"—an allusion to the potentially crippling dowry that an Indian bride's parents are expected to pay when the daughter gets married.... The result is an alarming shortage of young Indian women and a growing population of young Indian men with little prospect of finding a wife.

The article continues:

The war against baby girls has spread to South Korea, Singapore and Taiwan, to the former Soviet republics of Armenia, Azerbaijan and Georgia and even to Asian-American communities in the United States. And if you think that the antidote to this "gendercide" is modernization, better living standards and more education, think again.

According to the *Times of London,* in a story published in 2007, it is not India's poorest but its richest who are eliminating baby girls at the highest rate, regardless of religion or caste. According to the *Times,* "Delhi's leafiest suburbs have among the lowest ratio of girls to boys in India, while the two states with the absolute lowest ratio are those with the highest per-capita income: Punjab and Haryana.

"Similarly," says the *Times*, "in China, the higher a province's literacy rate or income per head, the more skewed its sexual disparities."

And in perhaps the most telling paragraph is this warning: "It is not material poverty that leads these cultures to blithely accept the killing of their very youngest girls. It is a poverty of values, an ancient prejudice that views daughters as a financial burden to be avoided, rather than a blessing to be cherished."

Gendercide Watch says female infanticide reflects the low status accorded to women in many societies around the world. The "burden" of accepting a woman into the family accounts for the high dowry rates in India. That, in turn, has led to an epidemic of female infanticide.

Typical also is China, where culture dictates that when a girl marries she leaves her family and becomes part of her husband's family. For this reason, Chinese peasants have for many centuries wanted a son to ensure there is someone to look after them in their old age. Having a boy child is the best (and often only) pension plan Chinese peasants can get. Baby girls, on the other hand, are even called "maggots in the rice."

Has Gendercide Arrived Here?

At this point in researching this book, I was prepared to conclude this chapter with a paragraph stating that there didn't appear to be any conclusive evidence that the practice of gendercide has taken root in any substantial way in Canada, when lo and behold I opened the *National Post* on the morning of April 12, 2010, to be confronted with the following headline: "Don't Reveal Sex of Fetuses, Medical Experts Urge."

The story, written by Tom Blackwell, says in part:

> Two Canadian medical experts are calling for new guidelines that would bar doctors from telling parents the sex of their fetus until late in a pregnancy, calling it a subtle way to curb the practice of sex selection.
>
> Writing in a major obstetrics journal recently, the bio-ethicist and doctor says physicians should delay imparting information on [the] baby's sex until it is too late for the woman to have an abortion with no questions asked.
>
> They admit it is unfortunate doctors should have to play such a role, but say it is unavoidable because Canadian law does not address the sex-selection phenomenon—or other aspects of abortion.
>
> "I think Canadians have a sort of visceral reaction to the idea that people would terminate a pregnancy based on gender alone," said Brendan Leier, a bio-ethicist at Edmonton's Stollery Children's hospital and co-author of the recommendations.
>
> One province, British Columbia, is already following the kind of policy he suggests.

The story goes on to say:

> Sex selection, fuelled by the widespread use of ultrasound scans that can often detect a fetus's gender, has been well documented in countries such as China and India.
> A 2006 study in the journal *Lancet*, co-authored by Prabhat Jha, head

of the University of Toronto's Centre for Global Health Research, used lopsided birth statistics in India to conclude that 10 million female fetuses had been aborted there in the previous two decades.

There is evidence, though less conclusive, that the same practice is common in North America among some immigrant populations. A 2003 analysis of Statistics Canada data by the *Western Standard* magazine found that communities in BC and Ontario with large South Asian populations had disproportionate numbers of male births.

It is especially apparent in the Sikh population of the west coast. In some Sikh households the birth of a girl is a cause for mourning, while baby boys are greeted with great celebration. The article continues:

A 2008 US study found that the ratio of boys to girls in families of Korean, Chinese or Indian background climbed steadily in favour of boys if the first child was a girl.

Mr. Leier and his co-author, Dr. Allison Thiele, an obstetrics and gynecology resident at the University of Saskatchewan, note that the official policies of professional groups such as the Society of Obstetrics and Gynecology of Canada (SOGC) condemn sex selection.

Dr. Alain Gagnon, an administrator with the BC Children and Women's Hospital in Vancouver admits that doctors in BC have, for several years, refused to divulge sex information until 20 weeks into the pregnancy.

These stories confirm my worst fears. Already some of the most repugnant aspects of some foreign cultures and practices have become well-established in Canada. How many more are we prepared to accept and bless under the guise of diversity and multiculturalism?

We have already turned a blind eye to polygamy in some ethnic communities, and you can be certain the practice of aborting female fetuses will continue to grow as more and more Asians and East Indians move into our cities. It is part of the deeply ingrained culture in those countries and it is naive to think that all those who come here will leave their beliefs and customs behind. Why would they? To them, it is normal, part of their culture.

Abortion is, after all, perfectly legal in this country—even if it does, in many situations, serve as a means of gendercide—and already the pro-abortionists are objecting to any suggestion that a woman should be curtailed from having an abortion for any reason at any time.

Joyce Arthur, co-coordinator of the Abortion Rights Coalition of Canada in Vancouver, wrote a letter to the *National Post* on April 15, 2010, in which she took issue with a *Post* column written earlier by Kelly McParland.

Arthur states:

> Kelly McParland makes the common mistake of trying to critique the pro-choice viewpoint through an anti-choice lens. He argues that to support a woman's right to choose, "you have to believe that a fetus is not human in the moral sense."
>
> This is incorrect. The pro-choice view is woman-focused and we take

no view on the fetus (or should not). The status and moral value of the fetus is moot because it's a matter of subjective personal opinion, and the only opinion that counts is the pregnant woman's.

No one wants to see abortions done for reasons of sex selection. But most pro-choice people do not want to ban the practice because that means removing personal autonomy in favour of society's values. Being pro-choice means supporting women's choices even when we don't agree with them—the hallmark of a truly free and democratic society.

Abortion is being scapegoated here. It's not abortion that leads to the problem of skewed sex ratios in China, India or even Canada. It's the low status of women, as well as the Indian dowry practice and the Chinese custom of passing the family line through the son.

She goes on to say:

Instead of trying to ban sex-selection abortion, governments should focus on educational campaigns to spark a cultural shift, introduce economic incentives to have daughters, and abolish discriminatory laws and policies that lead families to favour boys over girls.

Her letter is really quite interesting in that she makes it very clear that we should do nothing to stop gendercide in this country except through "sparking a cultural shift." Problem is, our multiculturalism laws tell us specifically we must accept all other cultures as equal and we can make no attempt to impose our values or our culture on anyone else.

I find if especially fascinating that Arthur states that the hallmark of a free and democratic society is supporting women's choices even when they clash with society's values. Then, in the same breath, suggests that we should somehow change the values of Chinese and Indian women who wish to abort females!

Some might suggest that it sounds just a tad racist. We should do nothing to change the values of Canadian women—only those women from India and China?

As for her argument that we should somehow introduce economic incentives to have daughters and abolish discriminatory laws and policies that lead families to favour boys over girls, in fact we already have employment equity laws in this country that favour the hiring of women over men in areas such as government, education, police and fire departments. More women than men now enter and graduate from our universities, more female doctors than men are now entering the profession; we even have more female soldiers serving on the front lines than ever before in our country's history.

Families in Canada who favour boys over girls do so for one reason and it has nothing to do with economics or discriminatory laws. Preferring boys to girls is purely cultural. Sadly, it is a cultural aspect that is being transplanted into the fertile, politically correct, multicultural soil of Canada.

So what's the next cultural "norm" that will take root here?

How do you feel about the widespread practice in some cultures of marrying off young girls to much older men? Are we ready for that dandy little cultural tradition?

Child Brides

Federal immigration officials say there's little they can do to stop "child brides" from being sponsored into Canada by much older husbands who wed them in arranged marriages abroad.

Top immigration officials say all they can do is reject the sponsorships of husbands trying to bring their child-brides to Canada. The men have to reapply when the bride turns 16. The marriages are permitted under Sharia law.

Muslim men, who are Canadian citizens or permanent residents often return to their homeland to wed a "child bride" in an arranged marriage in which a dowry is given to the girl's parents. Officials say some of the brides can be 14 years old or younger and are "forced" to marry. The practice occurs in a host of countries including Afghanistan, Iran, Pakistan and Lebanon.

(Tom Godfrey, "Muslim child brides on rise," Toronto Sun, March 11, 2010)

The phenomenon is also common in Yemen, as reported in an article by Mohammed Jamjoom, CNN, on April 9, 2010:

> A 12-year-old Yemeni bride died of internal bleeding following intercourse three days after she was married off to an older man, the United Nations Children's Fund said.
>
> The girl was married to a man at least twice her age, said Sigrid Kaag, UNICEF regional director for the Middle East and North Africa.
>
> Her death is "a painful reminder of the risks girls face when they are married too soon," Kaag said Thursday.
>
> Amal Basha, chairwoman of the Sisters Arab Forum for Human Rights, a Yemeni human rights group, identified the girl Friday as Elham Mahdi.
>
> "Elham was married on March 29th and died three days later" and lived in Yemen's Hajjah province, Basha said.
>
> The girl's death is the latest in a series of child marriage cases in Yemen, where the minimum age to tie the knot is still under debate.
>
> Frustrated by the recent revelation, a Yemeni government official called the case "a stark reminder that the practice of underage marriage must come to an end.
>
> "The government has been working tirelessly to cement the minimum marriage age but conservative parliamentarians have stood against it," said the official, who is not authorized to speak to the media. "Members of the conservative block need to step up to the responsibility of protecting the rights and freedoms of the young."

In September, a 12-year-old Yemeni girl forced into marriage died during childbirth. Her baby also died, according to the Seyaj Organization for the Protection of Children. Fawziya Ammodi was in labor for three days before she died of severe bleeding, said Ahmed al-Qureshi, president of the organization.

Child brides are common in Yemen, where the United Nations estimates that one in three girls are married before age 18. Most are married off to older men with more than one wife, according to a study by Sanaa University.

For the girl's parents, marriage means the daughters are no longer a financial or moral burden. Most times, parents get a promise from the husband to wait until the girl is older to consummate the marriage.

The issue of Yemeni child brides made headlines in 2008 when 10-year-old Nujood Ali was pulled out of school and married. Her husband beat and raped her within weeks of the ceremony. To escape, Nujood hailed a taxi—the first time in her life—to get to the central courthouse where she sat on a bench and demanded to see a judge. After a well-publicized trial, she was granted a divorce."

On April 24, 2010, ArabNews.com reported the following, written by Ahmad Al-Haj (AP):

Yemen's most influential Islamic cleric vowed on Saturday to gather a million signatures to protest a draft law banning child brides, in an increasingly vocal showdown against the country's weak government which needs the support of powerful religious leaders to hold onto power.

The issue of child brides in Yemen has attracted broad international attention, most recently earlier this month when a 13-year-old girl bled to death after her 23-year-old husband allegedly tied her down and forced her to have sex with him.

The cleric, Sheikh Abdul-Majid Al-Zindani, said, "...a ban on child brides threatens our culture and society and spreads immorality." Al-Zindani is Yemen's most powerful Islamic scholar and believed by the US to be a spiritual mentor of Osama Bin Laden.

Speaking at a conference at Iman University in the Yemeni capital Sanaa, Al-Zindani called on the dozens of clerics and Islamic law students in the crowd to oppose the draft law. "You have to gather a million signatures that supports the demands of the clerics," said Al-Zindani. "If the issue calls on us to gather a million protesters we'll organize it."

The practice of marrying young girls to much older men is widespread in Yemen, where one quarter of all females marry before they turn 15, according to a 2009 report by the country's Ministry of Social Affairs.

Once again, according to our multiculturalism laws, this is a cultural tradition that must be respected here. This is a culture that is equal to anything our ancestors provided for us. Or so we are supposed to believe!

One of the reasons that some MPs in Canada fought so hard and so long against raising the age of sexual consent from 14 to 16 was that they feared such a move would harm them in some ethnic communities.

Should Saudi Arabian Culture be Allowed Here?

Nazia Quazi and her fiancé Bjorn Singhal, saw each other Monday in Dubai for the first time in two years and they will be married as soon as they can sort out the paperwork. On Monday morning, Quazi, a Canadian who said her father had kept her in Saudi Arabia against her will for the better part of three years because he disapproved of Singhal, arrived in the United Arab Emirates with her mother, father and brother in tow.

(Jennifer Campbell, "Nazia reunited with fiancé," The Ottawa Citizen, *May 10, 2010)*

In 2007, Nazia Quazi, a 24-year-old Canadian woman, left her mother and brother in Ottawa and travelled to Saudi Arabia to visit her father and to do the Umrah, the Muslim pilgrimage to Mecca. When she arrived, her father, who did not approve of her fiancé, immediately took Nazia's travel documents and identification and until May of 2010 refused to let her leave. In very wealthy Saudi Arabia, fathers must make all decisions for their unmarried daughters, no matter their age or circumstance. The Saudis, who are supposed to be among the West's best friends, held Nazia captive in their country all that time. Only when the case obtained worldwide attention did Nazia's father change his mind and allow her to leave.

There are many, including some in this country, who would have you believe that things like stoning women to death, gendercide, floggings and forced childhood marriages are anomalies confined to backward, rural areas stricken with abject poverty.

We have dear friends who actually believe all the ills of the world, including abuse of women, would end if we could just eradicate poverty. They, like so many well-meaning but naive inhabitants of Canada's left wing, don't let facts get in the way of their ideology. As we have already seen, aborting and killing female fetuses and babies appears more common in the wealthy areas of India. Let's have a close look at how women are treated in one of the richest nations on earth—Saudi Arabia. Then ask ourselves, should we allow Saudi culture anywhere near Canada?

First and foremost is the fact that all human rights and laws in Saudi Arabia are based on Sharia religious laws dictated by the Saudi royal family. According to Amnesty International, Sharia imposes "gross human rights abuses against women." This includes, says the agency, "arbitrary arrest and detention…secret and grossly unfair trials; torture and cruel, inhuman or degrading treatment or punishment; and the use of the death penalty [through beheading]."

The full report, *Saudi Arabia: Gross human rights abuses against women*, can be found by googling "Amnesty International, Saudi Arabia."

The report is a mind-boggling chronicle of what life for women in Saudi Arabia entails. Women in Saudi Arabia are forbidden by law from driving cars, appearing in most public places without a male relative and are denied most jobs. In a 2000 United Nations report, it was estimated that only five per cent of Saudi women are in the workforce, almost all in so-called traditional female jobs.

In 2004, the UN Committee against Torture citied Saudi Arabia over the fact that punishment for relatively minor crimes includes floggings and the amputation of hands or feet. The Saudi delegation responded to the criticism by saying that these were "legal traditions" dating back to the inception of Islam 1,400 years ago.

Women are not allowed by law to mingle with men who are unrelated. They are not allowed to travel alone or enter government offices. They cannot leave the country unless accompanied by a male relative. Several Saudi female students will be admitted to Canadian universities in the next several years; each must be accompanied at all times by a male "minder."

The only exception to the rule concerning non-related men is when women have been accused of a crime. They are locked in a room and interrogated by men, which, Amnesty International says, is very intimidating for women unused to being in the company of male strangers. Women are often not allowed a lawyer.

Saudi religious police can order an arrest that often ends in torture if they feel the accused has not prayed at the right time or in the proper fashion.

Women are often arrested or beaten if their ankles or face are visible.

And perhaps worst of all, a woman can divorce a man under certain conditions and keep the children—but only for a while. The boy must be handed over to the father at age seven, the girl can stay with her mother only until she is nine. The mother is often left destitute, and very frequently is never allowed to see her children again.

United Nations and Amnesty International documents concerning the abuse of women in Saudi Arabia fill many pages; too many for me to relate here, but I think you get the message. For further information concerning the abuse of women in Saudi Arabia, the articles "Saudi Arabia: A justice system without justice" and "Saudi Arabia: A secret state of suffering" are available at www.amnesty.org.

Despite the overwhelming evidence of discrimination and even cruelty towards women, and their abysmal human rights record, the Saudis continue to be treated with kid gloves in Canada.

From 1984 until 2002, Saudi nationals could enter and leave any part of Canada without a visa. But immediately following 9/11, Canadian foreign affairs, immigration and security officials required Saudis to apply for entrance visas before coming to this country to study or work. The visas were valid for only 18 months.

But very quietly, the Saudis pulled strings and perhaps spent a bucketload of money and, lo and behold, in May of 2010 we learned that a new visa deal was worked out, providing all Saudis with visas that are good for five years with unlimited entrances and exists.

This is no small matter because, despite the tough visa requirements imposed in 2002, the number of Saudis entering Canada on entrance visas has skyrocketed in the past seven years. Last year, for example,

Canada granted entrance visas to 5,292 new Saudi students and 1,665 Saudi Arabian workers, compared to only 351 students and 199 Saudi workers in 2002.

Genital Mutilation

The American Academy of Pediatrics [AAP] has rescinded a controversial policy statement raising the idea that doctors in some communities should be able to substitute demands for female genital cutting with a harmless clitoral "pricking" procedure.

"We retracted the policy because it is important that the world health community understands the AAP is totally opposed to all forms of female genital cutting, both here in the US and anywhere else in the world," said AAP President Judith S. Palfrey.

The contentious policy statement, issued in April, had condemned the practice of female genital cutting overall. But a small portion of the statement suggesting the "pricking" procedure riled US advocacy groups and survivors of female genital cutting.

In the April statement, the AAP raised the idea that some physicians should be able to "prick" or "nick a girl's clitoral skin in order to "satisfy cultural requirements." The group likened the nick to an ear piercing.

On Thursday the group stated the group would not condone doctors providing any kind of "clitoral nick." The AAP also clarified nicking a girl or women's genitals is forbidden under a 1996 federal law banning female genital mutilation.

"I cried and told them how grateful I am," said Soraya Mire, a Somali filmmaker and survivor of female genital cutting. "Thank you for understanding us survivors and hearing our voices."

Equality Now, an international advocacy group fighting to end female genital cutting, echoed a similarly appreciative response.

"We welcome the AAP's decision to withdraw its 2010 policy statement on FGM," said Lakshmi Anantnarayan, a spokeswomen at Equality Now. "This is a crucial step forward in the movement to raise awareness about female genital mutilation."

Up to 140 million women and children worldwide have been affected by female genital cutting, according to the World Health Organization.

In the US, an estimated 228,000 women have been cut—or are at risk of being cut—because they come from an ethnic community that practices female genital cutting, according to an analysis of 2000 Census data conducted by the African Women's Health Center at Brigham and Women's Hospital.

(Stephanie Chen, "Pediatricians now reject all female genital cutting," CNN, May 27, 2010)

We don't have comparable data for Canada, but you can be certain female genital cutting is another traditional custom that is carried out in this country and, as certain cultural communities grow larger and more isolated, you can safely assume the practice will increase over time.

Ayaan Hirsi Ali, in both of her runaway bestselling books, *Infidel* and *The Caged Virgin*, is highly critical of Western nations for what she describes as deliberately overlooking aspects of the Muslim culture that oppress women. Her accounts of female genital mutilation, arranged marriages and domestic violence throughout the Middle East have shocked millions of readers and prompted several threats against her life. On more than one occasion she has been forced into hiding. (One of the knives plunged into Dutch filmmaker Theo van Gogh's chest had a note pinned to it threatening Hirsi Ali's life.)

Somali-born Hirsi Ali, named by *Time* magazine in 2005 as one of the 100 most influential people in the world, claims the Islamic vision is a caliphate society ruled by Sharia law that, among many other things, would have women stoned to death for adultery.

Hirsi Ali claims that when she was a little girl a female relative gouged her clitoris out with a piece of broken glass and that such practice continues to be widespread throughout the Muslim world. Hirsi Ali risked her life escaping from her country in order to avoid an arranged marriage to a man she detested, served in the Dutch parliament and finally, in order to escape death threats, moved to the United States.

Meantime, an investigation is still underway in St. Catharines to determine how widespread the culture of genital mutilation is in Ontario. It follows the conviction of a couple in that town who had their 11-year-old daughter's clitoris removed.

Nadia Badr, a leader in the Sudanese community in Ontario, says she's tried for years to change cultural views on female genital mutilation with little success. "Many men and women don't believe it is wrong," says Badr, "it's something that has happened in their culture for generations."

Hirsi Ali says in some Middle Eastern countries there is a widespread belief that if the clitoris is not removed it will grow to enormous lengths, hanging down between the girl's legs!

Sheema Khan, writing in the April 21, 2010, edition of the *The Globe and Mail* says, "The United Nations estimates that as many as 90 per cent of Egyptian women have undergone female genital mutilation."

All Cultures Are Not Equal

As many as 5,000 women and girls lose their lives—most at the hands of family members—in "honour killings" around the world each year, according to the United Nations.

Up to a dozen have died for the same reason in Canada in the last decade and it's happening more often, says Amin Muhammad, a psychiatrist [at Memorial University in Newfoundland] who studies honour killings.

"There are a number of organizations which don't accept the idea of honour killing; they say it's a Western-propagated myth by the media, but it's not true," he says. "Honour killing is here and we should acknowledge it, and Canada should take it seriously."

Kingston, Ontario, police are now investigating that [honour killing] as a motive in the deaths of three teenage sisters and an older female relative who were found in a car submerged in the Rideau Canal near

Kingston on June 30. The girls' mother, father and brother were arrested Wednesday and charged with first-degree murder."

(Shannon Proudfoot, "Rise in Canadian 'honour killings' should not be ignored: expert," National Post, *July 23, 2009)*

· · ·

"This is a lot more prevalent in North America than I had thought… It is the dirty laundry of the community." says Shelly Saywell, the producer of a film dealing with the parental abuse and honour killings of teen-aged girls in Canada as quoted by Margaret Wente in the *Globe and Mail,* May 8, 2010. The film, *In the Name of the Family,* has been widely acclaimed and has being screened for some Toronto high-school students.

· · ·

You can be as politically correct as you like. You can paper it over all you want, but the fact remains that equal rights and equal respect for women, as a matter of national policy and custom, are restricted to a relatively few western nations. Equal rights and respect for women are primarily Western values.

It is a dangerous myth, perpetrated by the multiculturalists, that all nations and cultures share the same core values, or at the very least, that all values are equally desirable.

Let me say it. All cultures do not share the same values. Furthermore, not all cultures are equally desirable.

Many of the cultures we are importing into Canada these days are repositories of ignorance, superstition, repression, cruelty and injustice, especially towards women.

There, I've said what very few in this country dare to say out loud!

I am not, for one moment, suggesting that all who come here from China, India, Yemen, Saudi Arabia or anywhere else subscribe to the belief that girls are of lesser value than boys.

There is no question that, historically, many immigrants from both India and China, in particular, have been among the most successful, productive and law-abiding of all newcomers. It is also true that Canadians of obvious East Indian or Asian ancestry very frequently finish at the top of their class in our schools and are winning many of the academic awards.

What I am saying is that it has become very obvious that immigration from all countries has changed drastically in recent years and we are at risk of implanting even more very undesirable cultural traditions firmly into this country if we continue to overwhelm the screening process with mass immigration. To further exacerbate the situation, we allow immigrants to settle into what amounts to ghettos that are little more than extensions of their birth country and do not insist they integrate into the Canadian mainstream.

After all, if some immigrants can come to Vancouver with the belief it is simply "little Shanghai," we shouldn't be surprised if some of Shanghai's less desirable qualities find a home here. If Surrey is just an extension of Punjab, small wonder the Punjabi conflict problems persist here. Interestingly enough, many of those in Punjab now claim there is a stronger and much more violent support for separation within the Sikhs of Canada than in India!

In fact, there is growing evidence of homegrown terrorism, racial strife on our campuses, honour killings, polygamy, gendercide and genital mutilation in some segments of our ethnic communities. Such evidence shows us that it's a totally different immigration world today than it was even 20 years ago.

The situation is so grave that for the first time in our history Canada has revised its citizenship study guide to warn newcomers that "barbaric cultural practices" such as honour killings will not be tolerated.

"In Canada, men and women are equal under the law," the new document says. "Canada's openness and generosity does not extend to barbaric cultural practices that tolerate spousal abuse, 'honour killings,' female genital mutilation or other gender-based violence. Those guilty of these crimes are severely punished under Canada's criminal laws."

The guide, released in the fall of 2009, is called *Discover Canada: The Rights and Responsibilities of Canadian Citizenship*. It is the first of its kind to denounce violence in the name of family honour.

only knows it's one giant mess the way it is now. Incredibly expensive, too!

Mind you, the odds are stacked against any of his proposals ever actually being implemented. Opposing him at every move is a veritable army of immigration lawyers, human rights activists, leftists, NGOs, most members of the opposition parties in parliament, and the thousands of people whose livelihoods depend upon maintaining and prolonging the chaos.

Let me give you just a brief overview of just how desperately bad the refugee situation is today.

In 2008, Auditor General Sheila Fraser reported that Canada had lost track of 41,000 refugee claimants. According to the RCMP, these claimants included at least 3,000 known criminals, including terrorists, murderers, warlords, torturers and thieves.

Some of the world's most hardened criminals have made their way to Canada and, amazingly enough, many were accepted as Canadian citizens; most of those ordered deported have simply disappeared into the ether someplace. They may be living next door to you!

Worse, Fraser found that there were 11,000 cases of refugees already in Canada who hadn't even been assigned to anyone for assessment. And incredibly, she found 30,000 refugees had outstanding arrest warrants for removal that had never been enforced. Some had been ordered deported seven years previously but the warrants never served!

In many cases we don't even know the proper names of refugee claimants since a common method of arriving here is to flush their travel documents down an aircraft's toilet. Or, more likely, hand it back to a human smuggler for recycling.

It is estimated that at the end of 2009, the number of "disappeared" refugee claimants totaled close to 60,000. And thanks to privacy laws, police cannot provide names, descriptions or pictures of those ordered deported who have pulled the disappearing act.

Most years, between 40,000 and 45,000 people arrive in Canada claiming refugee status. Up until 9/11 the bulk of those were admitted as Canadian citizens but even those rejected were seldom forced out. The approval rate in 1989, for example, was 90 per cent. One of the truly frightening aspects of this is the fact that following 9/11 the deputy director of CSIS, Jack Hooper, told a shocked Senate committee that only about 10 per cent of immigrants and refugees from Pakistan and Afghanistan received any security screening.

In 2009, there were 33,200 claims for asylum from people arriving here. Of those, 12,400 claims were approved. In practical terms, this means that most of the 20,800 not approved will go on our welfare rolls until their cases are either heard, or appeals are launched. It takes, on average, four and a half years to process a refugee claim. In the meantime, the refugee is provided free legal assistance, accommodation, health care, education and all other benefits afforded a bona fide Canadian citizen with the one exception being they cannot vote.

The estimated cost to taxpayers for each failed claim is $50,000. There is no estimate available of what it costs us to support those whose claims are slowly being processed. Keep in mind, refugee claimants are not supposed to work until granted landed immigrant status or otherwise receive a work permit. During the nearly five years it now takes to resolve a case, the claimant almost always is on welfare.

One of the reasons it takes so long to resolve a refugee claim is an incredible appeal process that often goes on for more than a decade.

Here are the steps available if a refugee claimant is turned down:

1. Seek judicial review in the Federal Court, which only considers mistakes in law. The success rate here is only about ten per cent.

2. Request a pre-removal risk assessment that examines whether rejected refugees would face torture or danger if deported. The success rate here is very low—only about four per cent.

3. File a humanitarian and compassionate review, arguing they would suffer unusual hardship if removed. Here the success rate is high—about 60 per cent.

4. Then, if all the three previous appeals have been turned down, you can ask the Federal Court to review the negative decisions in the three other appeals.

Some appellants have dragged this out for 20 or more years. All costs, of course, are borne by taxpayers!

This incredible rat's nest of trouble is all thanks to a far-left-wing Supreme Court Judge named Bertha Wilson. What she did to this country is hard to imagine.

The year is 1985. We don't have a refugee problem. Oh, being good Canadians we do welcome in a few thousand legitimate refugees every year. Real refugees—men, women and children who face violence, starvation, rape or torture in their native countries. Often they are victims of natural disasters or local wars.

Then it hits the fan!

Six Sikhs from India, all with the surname Singh, appear at the Supreme Court of Canada to appeal a deportation order issued by the Immigration Appeal Board.

All hell breaks loose! The country is never the same again.

The six Singhs tell the court they will be persecuted back in India if forced to return.

Every court in the land has thus far turned them down. But no other court boasted a Bertha Wilson on the bench.

Incredibly, Judge Wilson rules that the refugee system as it exists in 1985 violates the *Canadian Charter of Rights and Freedoms*, which she claims guarantees everyone on Canadian soil, including asylum seekers, the right to what she called fundamental justice.

In practical terms, what it means is that no matter how undesirable a person may be all they have to do is set one foot on Canadian soil and presto—they instantly become eligible for all the rights and privileges accorded any bona fide Canadian citizen, except for the right to vote. What it also means is that if they get themselves a good immigration lawyer at taxpayers' expense, they will be in the country for good with hardly any questions asked. Tens of thousands have done it and continue to do it.

The news spread like wildfire around the Third World. We might as well have posted huge signs on every tree and fence post in the messed-up parts of the world shouting: Send Canada your crooks, your thieves, your murderers, the people who have screwed up so badly nobody else wants them.

Finally, our government wakes up and four years later in 1989 establishes the Immigration and Refugee Board of Canada to deal with the mess. By that time, an astonishing 115,000 people, all claiming refugee status, have managed to set that one magic foot in our country and are claiming refugee status. We can't begin to handle the flood, so thousands are simply waved in without even having to submit their name.

Finally, Some Changes!

The plan announced in March 2010 by Immigration Minister Jason Kenney is the first attempt to streamline the system and, more importantly, screen out the bogus claims since Supreme Court Justice Wilson opened the refugee floodgates with her incredible ruling back in 1985.

The most contentious part of Kenney's proposal is that we identify so-called designated safe countries of origin from which we will not accept refugees but even here it seems we're not prepared to entirely shut the door. Those from the "safe country" list can still appeal to the Federal Court which, if past experience is any judge, can take years to process. It also remains to be seen which countries are deemed to be safe—that is, where democratic governments are in place and a stable system of law and order exists. Kenney has indicated he's talking about countries within the European Union, in Central America and Mexico.

The question whether, in fact, Mexico can correctly be deemed to be a "safe country" is being hotly debated. Peter Showler, a former chairman of the Immigration and Refugee Board who now teaches Advanced Refugee Law at the University of Ottawa, says that while some of Kenney's proposals please him, the "safe country" designation is going to be very difficult to obtain consensus on. Mexico, he says, is not a safe country.

This question is going to have to be resolved because today almost one third of all refugee claimants are coming from Mexico. Of the 34,000 claims for asylum in 2009, 9,296 came from Mexico, followed by Hungary (2,434), Colombia (2,300), Czech Republic (2,200), Haiti (1,600) and China (1,580).

A panel of public servants will examine the situation and make recommendations concerning the list of "safe" countries, but in the end it is a political decision that will have to be made by the Canadian government.

There is no question that if Kenney's proposals can actually be implemented it will greatly reduce the number of bogus refugee claims and, almost as importantly, greatly speed up the method of kicking the failed claimants out of the country. Most Canadians will also undoubtedly welcome the idea of going into refugee camps in war-torn and natural disaster-ravaged countries and rescuing at least 2,500 every year. Genuine refugees; what a concept!

The problem, of course, is that there is a huge and highly profitable immigration industry of lawyers, academics, leftist organizations, refugee advisors, people smugglers, false document providers, and ethnic groups that will fight tooth and nail against any attempt to lessen the chaos or speed things up. Less chaos in the refugee system—less delay—means less profit for those who are making fortunes from the whole mess and we will surely hear from plenty of them in the coming months.

Immigration expert Martin Collacott is more optimistic than I. He claims:

> What is clear is…that [Immigration Minister] Kenney has put forth a comprehensive and carefully thought out plan to deal with the chaos in our refugee determination system that has been festering for years. In doing so, he has included provision for enabling genuine refugees to settle in Canada and begin their new lives without the extended delays they now face. Given the challenges he will face in implementing his proposals, it may well be that at some stage he will have to revise some of them to make them completely workable. With his command of the issues and the resolve he has shown, to date, however, there is every likelihood that he will do his best to see the job through.

> (*Martin Collacott, "Reining in refugee chaos,"* National Post, *April 6, 2010*)

We will spend a whopping $540.7 million over the next five years trying to implement Kenney's new plan. I sure as heck hope it works!

In the meantime, the signs are still posted around the less desirable plots of real estate posing as nations declaring: Send us your bad guys, your killers, your thieves, thugs and mugs. Canada welcomes them all with open arms and cheque books at the ready. They obviously heard the message loud and clear in Sri Lanka.

Thank you Bertha Wilson and "progressives" everywhere!

Doctors Driving Cabs

"Have you ever met a cabbie who's not a doctor?" The question comes, only half jokingly, from a seatmate at a recent Ottawa Senators game. "I take a cab here to Scotiabank Place every game," he tells me "and I swear, every time I get an earful from a driver who claims he used to perform brain surgery back home some place in the old country, but here in Canada all they'll let him do is drive a taxi." He shakes his head. "Geez, you'd think it was Cuba here or something where doctors push bikes along the beach selling toothpaste and stuff."

He goes on like this for some time, a bit of fluffing up the truth for sure, but not entirely. Not all cab drivers are frustrated brain surgeons, but the truth of the matter is we know it's not all that uncommon because the facts stare us in the face. Immigrants arriving in Canada since the 1980s have not been doing nearly as those who arrived before we opened the floodgates.

It's all there in a study carried out by Statistics Canada called *Earnings inequality and earnings instability of immigrants in Canada.*

Lets have a look at some raw facts, gleaned from the 2006 Census:

- In 1980, recent-immigrant men earned 85 cents for every dollar earned by their Canadian-born counterparts. In 2005, recent-immigrant men earned only 63 cents compared to their Canadian-born counterparts.

- In 1980, recent-immigrant women earned 85 cents for every dollar earned by their Canadian-born counterparts. In 2005, recent-immigrant women earned only 56 cents compared to their Canadian-born counterparts.

- In 2005, recent-immigrant men holding a university degree earned only 48 cents for each dollar their university educated Canadian-born counterparts did.

- In 2005, about 30 per cent of university educated immigrant men worked in Canadian jobs that required no more than a high school education—more than twice the rate of those born in Canada.

Rene Morissette, lead analyst with Statistics Canada, says the trend started in 1980 when immigrants began to see their earnings level fall even though their education levels "grew remarkably" compared to those of Canadian-born workers.

That observation is especially revealing because, since the 1980s, Canada has placed increased importance on education, believing this would improve an immigrant's chance of employment. Just the opposite happened. Almost in lockstep with Canada's requirements for better educated immigrants, we see the wage gap grow wider between recent immigrants and Canadian-born workers.

So what happened?

Well, what happened is that in the 1980s we opened the floodgates to large numbers of immigrants from non-traditional sources. In other words, instead of the ratio being about four immigrants from Western nations to every immigrant from non-Western countries, we reversed the situation, so that today for every one immigrant from a Western democracy, about four are arriving from non-Western nations. And, very obviously, the immigrant of today who is creating this "New Canada" just isn't doing as well; not nearly as well, for the most part, as immigrants who arrived here a few years ago. It certainly doesn't bode well for this "New Canada" that the "progressives" are eagerly awaiting.

And the question remains: Why are immigrants today not doing nearly as well financially as those who arrived prior to 1980?

The most thorough examination of the declining fortunes of recent immigrants was carried out in 2005 by Garnett Picot and Arthur Sweetman of Statistics Canada. They found three main reasons for the growing wage gap.

"The main reason," they say "is the changing characteristics of today's immigrants, including country of origin, language and education."

To put it more bluntly, many immigrants arriving these days can't speak English or French properly and while they may appear to be well-educated, many employers just don't believe that an education acquired in the homeland of many newcomers comes close to Canadian standards.

Picot and Sweetman also found that many employers in Canada are suspicious about the work experience declared by recent immigrants.

To sum up, Canadian employers do not value foreign education or foreign work experience, and also there's often a language problem.

Let me quote directly from the Picot and Sweetman report entitled *The deteriorating economic welfare of immigrants and possible causes: Update 2005*.

> Like previous research, the paper concludes that the earnings gap at entry has increased for immigrants entering Canada during the 1990s, as compared to those of the 1970s. Furthermore, the gap in the low-income rate has been increasing. The rate of low income has been rising among immigrants (particularly recent immigrants) during the 1990s, while falling among the Canadian-born. The rise in low-income rates among immigrants was widespread, affecting immigrants in all education groups, age groups, and from most source countries (except the "traditional source regions"). Immigrants with university degrees

were not excluded from this rise in low-income rates, in spite of the discussion regarding the rising demand for more highly skilled workers in Canada. As a result of both rising low-income rates among immigrants, and their increasing share of the population, in Canada's major cities virtually all of the increase in the city low-income rates during the 1990s was concentrated among the immigrant population.

Translation: Almost all of those living below the so-called poverty line in our major cities are recent immigrants. It's a fact almost totally ignored during any discussion of poverty or low-income earners in Canada.

Patrick Grady, an economic consultant with Global Economics Ltd., and a former senior official with the Federal Department of Finance and Bank of Canada, writes an interesting chapter in the book *The Effects of Mass Immigration on Canadian Living Standards and Society.* He says: "There is growing evidence that Canadian employers are not just being stupid. They have reasonable grounds to discount the value of foreign education. The disconnect between education and skills for many immigrants from third-world countries seems to be a definite factor explaining the poorer earning performance."

He goes on to list a number of economic studies that indicate the education obtained in many foreign countries is simply not as good as it is in Canada. He cites the recent International Adult Literacy Survey that identified a 45-percentage point difference between average skill-level test scores of immigrants with no Canadian education and those of the native born. Another study, using the same test scores, found, "a learning gap of 3.0 years for recent immigrants and 2.1 years even for those whose first language was English or French. That is enough to make a foreign university graduate with a pass degree equivalent to a Canadian high school graduate."

Read My Lips: It's Not Racism!

Please, given these studies, and many other with similar conclusions, can we stop claiming it's racism that is impeding recently arrived immigrants? You can hardly open a newspaper these days or watch television news without grave head-shaking assurances from countless "experts" that the reason many newcomers can't seem to drag themselves out of poverty is nothing but pure and simple racism. It's all our fault, is the constant mantra.

The "experts" all would have us believe that, for some unexplained reason, employers who a few years ago welcomed immigrants with open arms have now suddenly all become racists. Pure nonsense, of course. Many studies, including those conducted by the Chrétien Federal Liberal government, have concluded that essentially a university degree from most of the countries now supplying us with immigrants is roughly the equivalent of a Canadian high school diploma. So if today's newly arrived immigrant with a university degree is earning high school wages it's not racism, it's just common sense.

And, by the way, the next time you hear one of these "experts" labelling Canadians as racists over this issue of immigrant low income, ask them to explain this please: Immigrants who obtain their university education in Canada do just as well economically as native-born Canadians!

The Welfare Burden

In May 2010, Andrew McIntosh, writing for the QMI Agency, reported that Mohamed Omary, a citizen of both Canada and Morocco, and a father of four, had collected welfare since arriving in this country more than 20 years ago. The cheques arrived even while he was visiting such places as France, Germany, Holland, Bosnia, Croatia, Slovenia and Turkey, as well as his native country, Morocco. Omary is suing the Attorney General of Canada, CSIS and the RCMP for a million dollars, claiming Canadian police tipped off Moroccan authorities that he was returning there, where he was then apparently imprisoned for a while. Police questioned him concerning his relationship with at least six terrorists. Omary claims that his detention in Morocco cost him lost income—his welfare cheques!

The intent of immigration is to benefit Canada. Or at least that should be the intent, and there is no question that up until the past two decades immigration has been of great benefit to this country.

Those in our vast "immigration industry" claim the benefits continue, but they would be very hard-pressed to prove it.

Flooding Canada with some 300,000 immigrants and refugee claimants every year, along with more than a quarter of a million foreign workers and 79,000 foreign students, places an incredible stress on such things as the country's health services, educational facilities, policing, social services, housing, and infrastructure. The welfare rolls take a terrible pounding but what is just as disturbing is the number of immigrants who are living below what Statistics Canada calls the poverty line. Many believe that this so-called poverty line is not a true reflection of poverty, but nonetheless it does provide a baseline to make comparisons and gauge just how poorly recent immigrants are doing.

Here are figures that illustrate very graphically how badly our immigration policy has been serving our country and our immigrants since 1980 :

- Before 1961, only 6.8 per cent of our immigrant population lived below the poverty line.

- By 1980 that figure climbed to 8.2 per cent.

- From 1981 to 1990 the rate went to 17.2 per cent.

- From 1996 until 2001 (the last year for which we have figures) the number of immigrants living below the poverty line had skyrocketed to an astonishing 41.2 per cent. Since the trend of higher unemployment for immigrants has steadily increased during the past decade, you can be certain that very disturbing figure has not declined.

- In comparison, 11.2 per cent of non-immigrants are living below the poverty line.

What is also very important is to see a breakdown of the low-income numbers as they relate to countries of origin.

- Between 1996 and 2001, immigrants from the US did by far the best in this country. Only 23.2 per cent of American immigrants were living below the poverty line.

- The rate was 33.7 per cent for immigrants from Europe.

- The rate for immigrants from Asia was 44.6 per cent.

- Fully 48.8 per cent of immigrants from Africa lived below the poverty line.

(All figures from Statistics Canada.)

Historically, immigrants, on a per capita basis, sucked up far less in welfare and other benefits than native-born Canadians because most of them were able to find jobs and many were not eligible for various forms of social services, including Old Age Security.

That picture has changed drastically and the most recent Census (2008) shows us that today, on a per capita basis, immigrants are eating up far more of our welfare dollars and other social benefits than those born in this country. Just one more illustration of how incredibly screwed up our immigration system has become since we opened the floodgates.

In his book *Who Gets In: What's wrong with Canada's immigration program–and how to fix it* author Daniel Stoffman claims:

> The expansion of family-class immigration over the past 20 years is the main reason the economic performance of immigrants has declined. Family-class immigrants need meet no criteria of skills or education; they can come even if they are illiterate in their own language. And so recent immigrants earn less, pay less tax, have higher unemployment rates and make more use of welfare than previous cohorts of immigrants.

Stoffman makes a very important observation when he says:

> Less than a quarter of Canada's immigration intake is selected on the basis of skills and education. The government pretends otherwise by including accompanying immediate family members in the independent category, bringing the official total of skilled immigrants to 60 per cent. This figure is misleading, though, for it includes a preponderance of spouses and small children, few of whom can claim to be skilled. More than three-quarters of immigrants, in short, need meet no educational criteria at all [sic]. ...plenty of uneducated, unskilled newcomers will continue to arrive, regardless of changes to the points system.

Many studies indicate he is at least partially correct in his conclusions, although other factors, which we have already outlined, are also involved. However, Stoffman makes some interesting observations when he says:

> Immigration policy, with its emphasis on family reunification, increases the supply of unskilled labour. Unskilled workers were already ill paid before the Mulroney-Chrétien immigration policy made matters worse for them. Is it in the national interest to make our poorest citizens poorer? Is this one of the things we want our immigration program to achieve? …workers impoverished by this policy should have a chance to offer opinions, based on a frank disclosure of costs and benefits.

> Such disclosure has never been made. In Canada, it's considered rude to even mention the costs of immigration. George Orwell pointed out that "at any given moment there is an orthodoxy, a body of ideas which, it is assumed, all right-thinking people will accept without question. It is not exactly forbidden to say this, that or the other, but it is 'not done' to say it, just as in mid-Victorian times it was 'not done' to mention trousers in the presence of a lady."

> That describes precisely the debate over immigration in Canada. The "right-thinking" version is that immigration is good and more immigration is better. Immigration brings only benefits. To suggest that there might be negative consequences is in the worst taste; it's "not done."

Stoffman goes on to ask:

> …if Canada does not need immigration, why accept negative consequences? Why accept a program that endangers the safety of the

Canadian people? Innocence is dangerous; we cannot afford it. At the very least, the benefits of immigration should outweigh the costs. They no longer do. That is why Canada's immigration program desperately needs to be overhauled.

That's the sixty-four thousand dollar question isn't it? Mass immigration and multiculturalism, as we can easily see, is not working for Canada and it's not working for most new immigrants, so why are we doing it?

The Great Myth

Senior citizens may soon outnumber children in Canada, according to a Statistics Canada projection.

The projection, released yesterday, says the Canadian population will reach more than 43.8 million in 2036—up from 33.7 million in 2009—if the population continues a medium-growth trend, which is based on consistent fertility, mortality and immigration trends. A high-growth scenario, which would see higher trends in all three categories, suggests Canada's population could jump to nearly 47.7 million.

For the first time, the senior population is expected to outnumber that of children under the age of 15 at some point between 2015 and 2021. The actual date depends on Canada's type of growth scenario. The federal agency expects the number of seniors to reach between 9.9 million and 10.9 million in 2036, representing a drastic spike from 2009 numbers, which reported 4.7 million seniors in Canada. By contrast, the population of children under the age of 15 is projected to register between 5.7 million and 8.2 million in 2036. There were 5.6 million children in that demographic in 2009.

(Bradley Bouzane, "Seniors may soon outnumber children," Canwest News Service, May 27, 2010)

But, you may say, we've got to have lots of immigrants. We need them desperately to provide the workforce for the aging population we keep hearing so much about.

If we don't leave the floodgates open for immigrants, you ask, who are going to be the worker bees out there fixing the roads, making cars and beer, picking strawberries and paying taxes so all the seniors and the retirees can continue to get their pensions? It sounds like a powerful argument, but it is simply not valid.

The belief that immigration is the answer to our low fertility rate and aging workforce is a great myth most of us have come to believe. It's a myth so powerful that, as a nation, we are about to abandon the ship that has served us so well and clamber aboard a foreign vessel headed we know not where, manned by a crew of often feuding strangers, most of whom speak a language we cannot understand!

Until I began researching this book, I confess I too believed we needed large numbers of immigrants to ensure a future workforce. The argument seems to make sense. We all know Canada's fertility rate has fallen well below the replacement level. We also know, as a society, we're getting older so why wouldn't we believe that the only thing to save us is mass immigration?

But then, it's really not that long ago that most of the world's finest minds "knew" the earth was flat and the sun made a daily trip around it. Science and logic finally rescued us from those delusions; the same kind of science and logic that has once again revealed the truth, this time about the folly of mass immigration.

It was Copernicus who gave us the news that the earth was not the centre of the universe. Since he's not around these days, we turn to the C.D. Howe Institute to provide the scientific evidence concerning the ability of mass immigration to replace the children we aren't having anymore.

"*De revolutionibus orbium coelestium*" was the title of Copernicus's epic discoveries about the sun. That, roughly translated, means "On the revolutions of the celestial spheres." The C.D. Howe Institute's findings concerning immigration are somewhat more prosaically entitled *Faster, Younger, Richer? The Fond Hope and Sobering Reality of Immigration's Impact on Canada's Demographic and Economic Future*.

And indeed, it is sobering.

The study, published in late-2009, is authored by Robin Banerjee, a former policy analyst at the C.D. Howe Institute, and William B.P. Robson,

President and Chief Executive Officer of the Institute. Their conclusion is as follows: "More and younger immigrants cannot, on their own, offset the impact of low past fertility on Canadian workforce growth, old-age dependency, and incomes per person. Later retirement, higher fertility, and faster productivity growth are more powerful tools to ease the stress of demographic change on Canadian living standards."

The report goes on to say: "For Canadians to expect more and younger immigrants to counteract the effects of low past fertility on workforce growth and aging would be a serious mistake. While immigration has been a key driver of Canadian population growth, it cannot, on its own, offset demographic trends that threaten our future living standards."

Further shattering any delusions we may still possess, the authors go on to say: "Current fertility and immigration rates, moderately rising life expectancy, and historical productivity growth can be expected to depress workforce growth, boost the ratio of Canadians 65 and over to those of working age (the old-age dependency ratio), and depress growth in incomes per person. Despite some popular commentary, offsetting or even noticeably mitigating these trends would require unrealistic increases in immigration."

Translation: If we don't make some serious changes very shortly, we are going to have fewer workers paying taxes to support more and more older Canadians, but immigration is not the answer.

The study, which was very extensive and involved computer projections utilizing Statistics Canada figures, arrived at several more very shocking conclusions.

For example, in order to maintain the present ratio of about five taxpayers for every pensioner, the number of immigrants would have to shoot up to unbelievable and totally unattainable levels.

One estimate shows that in order to maintain a five-to-one ratio by the year 2050, Canada's population would have to be 210 million and the intake in that year alone would have to be an astonishing seven million. When you stop and really think about it you can understand why. After all, immigrants age at the same pace as everyone else and, like other Canadians, are eligible to receive social benefits in retirement.

Another aspect of the study they conducted suggested restricting immigration only to those aged 20. Even that would have a minimal effect on maintaining the five-to-one ratio.

Interestingly enough, similar studies in the US came to exactly the same conclusions. In order to determine if immigration could ensure the five-to-one ratio of workers to retirees in the US, the UN conducted a very thorough study that dumbfounded them. That study concluded that in order to maintain the five-to-one ratio the US would have to accept immigrants at about ten times the current level; that is about 11 million annually. If they did that the American population by 2050 would be in excess of one billion—four times greater than it is today.

In 1991, the Organization for Economic Co-operation and Development (OECD) examined immigration data since the Second World War for seven countries, including Canada. Its study confirms the findings of Banerjee and Robson. Immigration, even of younger people, will do little or nothing to reduce the average age in a country. The OECD's conclusions are, in fact, rather shocking. Even the kind of mass immigration experienced in Canada since 1945 has succeeded in lowering the average age of Canadians by less than one year.

Very clearly, immigration isn't going to supply us with enough workers to ensure that our pension cheques don't bounce in the future.

Does this mean the situation is hopeless? Should we just forget about any kind of government support in our dotage?

Not at all. There are plenty of answers; in fact there may not be much to worry about at all.

All the studies give a clear indication the problem is not nearly as serious as many would have us believe and, even more hopefully, there are a number of relatively easy things we can do to maintain a reasonable balance between workers and retirees.

Banerjee and Robson conclude that if we would just do the following three things all our future needs for working taxpayers would be met:

1.   Delay the age of retirement to at least age 70.

2.   Encourage higher fertility rates.

3.   Increase productivity by at least one per cent per year.

I believe we have some other options as well but before we get into solutions it might be a good idea to determine if, in fact, we really do have a problem or, at the very least, examine just how serious and immediate it is.

For the full Banerjee/Robson report, google "C.D. Howe Institute Immigration (Banerjee/Robson)."

Is There Really a Problem?

> Ontario's universities plan to cut as many as 1,000 spots in their teacher-training programs over the next couple of years, but it remains unclear if such a move will eliminate a growing surplus of new graduates entering the profession.
>
> For every two new teachers certified each year, there remains only one job in the province, pushing many to find part-time work, move overseas or leave the profession altogether.
>
> John Milloy, Minister of Training, Colleges and Universities, said yesterday that cutting back the number of graduates will help.
>
> *(Caroline Alphonso and Kate Hammer, "Up to 1,000 spots to be cut from teachers' ed," The Globe and Mail, April 19, 2010)*

The news didn't come as any great shock to me, because late in 2009 and again in early 2010 I began to receive phone calls and emails from young Ontarians who had recently graduated from teachers' colleges only to discover that there were absolutely no jobs available in their chosen profession and no prospect of them in the near future.

Small wonder the province is cutting back on the number of teacher training spaces. It turns out that each year for the past number of years, Ontario has been churning out about 13,000 graduates from various teachers' colleges. This is about twice the number needed to fill vacancies because, on average, only about 6,500 teachers either retire in Ontario or move on to other jobs each year. Compounding the problem are claims that even when substitute teachers are required, it is usually the older, retired ones who get the call to come in and help out for a day or two. Seldom do recent teaching graduates receive a similar opportunity.

Now let me tell you about phone calls and emails I have been receiving for many years from the owners of local garages, contractors, plumbers, and welders, sheet metal, electrical and machine shop owners and operators desperate to find trained help. A good friend had to cancel an advertising contract with me because it was just too successful. "Lowell," he told me, "I just can't handle all the business. I'd like to, but I just can't find nearly enough trained plumbers, no matter what I am prepared to pay. People hear your ads and get furious when I tell them I can't help them out for at least two days, probably longer. Maybe what I should be doing is advertising for some skilled plumbers!"

So let me ask you the obvious question. Do we need to import thousands of trades people from China, India, Pakistan or Mexico, or do we just need to make sure we are training people here for jobs that actually exist? I'm not suggesting that's the only answer to labour shortages or that all those 13,000 trained teachers we produce each year would be suitable as skilled tradespeople, but you can bet your bottom dollar that more than a few of them would have taken trades courses if they had known highly paid unionized jobs would be begging for them the day they graduated!

Consulting with local business to better determine what jobs are most likely to be opening up in the future is one step we should be taking, not just to reduce the number of immigrants required, but to ensure that employers have enough skilled workers to keep their businesses booming and the workers have enough well-paid jobs waiting for them when training is complete.

By the way, it's not just in the skilled trades that we have very badly misjudged the needs of employers. Even today with the industry greatly scaled back, one of the first things you often notice when you walk into a high-tech office or plant is the large number of employees who very obviously have come here from other countries.

Do we really need to import tens of thousands of workers to fill all those Canadian jobs, or do we just need to do a better job of making sure we are equipping our young people with skills that the workplace actually needs today and will need tomorrow?

And there's another question. Why in the world are we bringing in about a quarter of a million immigrants every year, plus about the same number of temporary workers, while our unemployment rate remains in the eight per cent range? It must be obvious to all but the most thick-headed that this country doesn't have a shortage of workers—if anything, it has a shortage of workers trained for the jobs that actually exist. We import tens of thousands of people from overseas, supposedly to fill vacant jobs in Canada, while tens of thousands of young Canadians are unemployed because we trained them for the wrong jobs.

And then, of course, there is the other problem—far too many of our able-bodied young people choose to stay on welfare rather than take a job they feel is beneath them. A change similar to the Mike Harris idea of "workfare" would probably flush more than a few of these lazy bozos off their comfortable couches and out into the work-a-day world. I know, I know, to suggest anything like that is politically incorrect! Just so happens it's also true. A quick visit to the Human Resources and Skills Development Canada website tells the tale—the numbers are there for all to see.

And think of this: If employers don't know that they can get all the workers they want from places like China or India or Mexico do you suppose they might work a bit harder at convincing governments to provide them with trained Canadian workers and get some of our welfare friends out into the harvesting fields? Some employers might even do a bit more training of their own.

There's another factor that indicates maybe we are worrying about nothing regarding low fertility rates and an aging workforce in Canada.

Stoffman, co-author of *Boom, Bust and Echo*, points out that a large group of young workers is just now starting to enter the workforce. "These," he says, "are the baby-boom echo, the offspring of the boomers. They were born between 1980 and 1995; at 6.5 million they are the second largest population cohort in Canada after the boomers themselves."

Stoffman says a steady stream of boomer-echos will be looking for their first job between now and 2015, and then asks: "Why make their entry into the labour force more difficult by bringing in armies of competing workers from abroad?"

Why, indeed!

This Makes No Sense

Actually we don't have to wait another day to see a steady stream of boomer-echos and others having a very difficult time finding a job.

A steady stream is hardly the appropriate phrase to describe what is happening today in Canada. A broken-dam tidal wave is a more apt description of the job hunters today. Not tomorrow—not in 2015— but today.

You may shake your head in total disbelief as you read this; it certainly shook me and my editors. So, as I sometimes advise radio listeners when I'm about to reveal something I believe is astonishing on the air, please sit down. If you're on any kind of medication have the pills at the ready. Here goes:

According to Statistics Canada, as of May 2010, 1,498,300 people were unemployed in Canada. Yes, you are reading it right. Figures for May 2010 show that one million, four hundred and ninety-eight thousand, three hundred people were looking for jobs in this country.

Which surely begs this question: Why in the world are we importing another 250,000 immigrants, to say nothing of 30,000 or 40,000 thousand refugees, a quarter of a million temporary workers, and 79,000 foreign students this year and every year?

Is this something that makes sense to you?

We've got nearly 1.5 million Canadians looking for work and we flood the country with another half million or so immigrants, refugees and temporary workers, at least half of whom will either have to find jobs or collect welfare?

This sure doesn't make much sense to me.

The argument from those who support mass immigration is that new Canadians create jobs. Undoubtly they do, but the problem is (there are plenty of studies that prove this), with rare exception, the number of jobs they create is equal to the number of jobs they hold.

If, in fact, immigration creates more jobs than the newcomers occupy, then Canada's unemployment rate should decline as we bring in more and more workers and their families. But this is just not the case.

If you examine historical unemployment rates (google "unemployment rate Canada/historical") you will see that there is absolutely no evidence that immigration has lowered the country's unemployment rate at any time. The charts show that until the floodgates were opened wide in 1991, there were substantial intake fluctuations from year to year, depending upon events such as wars, recessions and, of course, the Great Depression, but nowhere can you find any indication whatsoever that immigration has had any effect on our unemployment rate. Certainly not in modern times.

As a matter of fact, if you look back to the figures for 2007 you will find that while the Canadian unemployment rate of six per cent was about as low as it had been in recent years, it was still higher than the G7 average of 5.6 per cent unemployment. Since Canada has by far the highest per capita intake of immigrants in the world, you would assume that if immigrants really do create more jobs than they occupy, this country would have by far the lowest unemployment rate among industrialized nations. As I have already stated, this is just not the case.

Until Mulroney, and then Chrétien, we had the good sense in this country to cut back on immigration when times got tough here. As I noted earlier, between 1983 and 1985, during the height of a serious recession, Trudeau reduced immigration levels by more than half (below 90,000) for three straight years. However, during the recession we are just now recovering from, immigration slackened off not one bit. In fact, even as more than two million Canadians were looking for work in 2008 and again in 2009, we still kept the immigration taps wide open at the rate of close to a quarter of a million newcomers each year.

So I ask again: Does any of this make any sense at all?

Of course it makes no sense, but nonetheless as a nation we continue to keep the immigration floodgates cranked wide open and for the most part we still believe that's the only way we can be assured that there'll be enough workers around to pay the taxes to keep our pension cheques from bouncing.

It's the old story of "don't confuse me with the facts!"

Making Sense of It

There's no question the problem of an aging population isn't nearly as serious as the supporters of mass immigration would have us believe. Don't forget that thousands of highly paid jobs are at stake if we reduce the number of immigrants coming into the country. The more that those living off the avails of the "immigration industry" can convince us that only mass immigration can stave off a fate worse than death the more their incomes are protected and the greater the chances their friends are hired.

Very clearly, we can easily do a much better job of educating and training our young people for jobs that actually exist or will exist. And it would only take a bit of tough love to get a few hundred thousand young able-bodied Canadians away from their TVs and cases of two-fours and out into the workforce. Mike Harris did it once in Ontario, and I have no doubt that as taxes continue to skyrocket we'll find another politician with enough guts to tell the young bums to "get a haircut and get a real job."

But it's obvious we've got to consider some other approaches, so let's examine the three solutions suggested in the C.D. Howe Institute study authored by Banerjee and Robson that said the only way to counter the aging population factor is to raise the age of retirement to 70, increase productivity at least one per cent a year and encourage higher fertility rates.

Postpone Retirement

The first part of the solution—raising the retirement age perhaps as high as 70—is a no-brainer. We're living longer and healthier today than ever before. There's more than a little truth to the claim that today's 75 is yesterday's 60. Well, maybe yesterday's 65, at the very least.

The fact is, this process has already begun with more and more people working well past 65, sometimes out of necessity, but often by choice.

By the time you read this I'll be 74 and have no intentions of slowing down. Not even a tad! Quite possibly the most successful politician in the country today is the Mayor of Mississauga, Hazel McCallion, who, as she closes in on 90, tells me she fully intends to run for office again.

And keep in mind that Churchill was 71 when he accepted the surrender of Nazi Germany.

Not everyone will be able to continue working until the age of 70 or beyond and no doubt some will choose not to. Already you can see that the push of working past the traditional retirement age of 65 is well underway.

In France, for example, thousands took to the streets in the spring of 2010 to protest government plans to increase the retirement age from 60 to 62.

In England, the coalition government has announced they want to raise the retirement age to a whopping 70 years of age over the next few decades.

The Danes are examining a process whereby retirement age will be linked to life expectancy and the pension age will rise in Denmark from 65 to 67 by 2027.

Greece has indicated it will ban early retirement (some government workers retire at 50) and increase the average retirement age there from 61 to 63 by 2015.

Germany, which today has by far the strongest economy in the European Union, took retirement-age action back in March of 2007 when it announced that anyone born after 1964 will have to wait until they are 67 in order to qualify for a government pension. The Bundestag (German Federal government) has also approved legislation designed to attract people born after 1945 (baby boomers) back into the labour market.

And the move to increase the age at which government pensions kick in is not confined to Europe.

In March of 2010, Illinois raised the retirement age for new state workers from as low as 55 all the way up to 67.

Two months later, California Governor Arnold Schwarzenegger raised the retirement age for state workers by five years and new legislation requires current workers to contribute more of their salaries into their own retirement accounts. Voters in many California cities will be voting later in 2010 on whether to increase retirement ages and cut pension benefits for municipal government employees.

And even more telling, President Obama's deficit commission is very seriously considering raising the retirement age for federal employees. Currently in the US, workers can start collecting reduced benefits at 62 with full benefits available at 66. Already a law has been passed by the Obama administration setting the full retirement age at 67 for those born after 1960.

One thing that is interesting to note is that the average American employee today works eight months longer than the average Canadian. The average retirement age for both men and women in the US is 65.8, compared to 65 in Canada.

There are a number of things the Canadian government could and should do to encourage us to work longer.

To begin with, if the retirement age is going to be boosted to 70, then the opportunity of contributing to an RRSP should be available until that age. As things stand now, those who work past the age of 65 are not afforded the same tax advantages as those under the age of 65. This is wrong. Other tax changes may have to be made. If the age of retirement is increased, we may have to delay the income-splitting provisions for seniors who work until the age of 70 and the age at which you can begin collecting your Old Age Security pension will likely have to be boosted.

According to the C.D. Howe report the simple act of increasing the age of retirement to 70 would go a long way to making us much less dependent upon immigrants to supply us with tax-paying workers. We can let the economists figure out the fine print and the sooner the better.

Susan McDaniel, director of the Prentice Institute for Global Population and Economy at the University of Lethbridge, says there is absolutely no need to panic. She's quoted in the May 26, 2010, edition of *The Globe and Mail* as saying: "Some of the mistake [concerning this business of an aging population] is that people, including policy people, see people who are 85 needing health care now, therefore thinking that people 20 years from now will need the same thing. But people who are 85 now were born in a time when smoking was chic, they sometimes went through the Depression—they're an entirely different person."

When today's baby boomers reach the age of 85 they will, on average, be a lot healthier, a lot more active, and won't require the same kind of health care that we see with people of that age today.

Monica Boyd, professor of sociology at the University of Toronto, agrees. "Not only are the future elderly not going to be a drain on the system," she says, "they will also be contributing, productive members of the economy. Many elderly people are choosing not to retire right away and many are able to work until they're much older as jobs move from labour-based to technology based."

If you really stop and think about it, the fact is many so-called elderly people today are living lifestyles that are much healthier, much more active and much more productive than those of previous generations. We are living longer, yes, but overall we are living much healthier lives and the point being made by more and more demographers is that we are worrying far too much about soaring health care costs and not having enough taxpayers to support the system. Many of the taxpayers supporting the system today are at an age that, in past generations, were considered too old, too frail and too sick to contribute, and every indication is that this trend of prolonged good health will continue.

It's just one more reason to again ask the question: Why are we importing more than half a million people into this country every year when we are seeing, to a large degree, that it is the newcomers, not the elderly, who are placing an increasingly heavy burden on the public purse.

Let's All Work Just a Bit Harder

The second solution, increasing Canadian productivity by at least one per cent a year, is surely a goal we should aim for, regardless of the immigration situation.

Productivity (how much an economy produces per hour of work and the number one way we determine our standard of living) in this country has always lagged behind that of the US, despite NAFTA (The North American Free Trade Agreement).

The latest figures from Statistics Canada indicate that the average Canadian worker produces only 82 per cent as much per hour as his or her counterpart in the US. To widen that gap even further is the fact that the average American works longer hours than the average Canadian. The good news is that the gap has narrowed somewhat since the 1950s, although that narrowing did slow down somewhat in the mid-1980s—at just about the time we began to accept the bulk of our immigrants from non-European countries.

Patrick Grady, co-founder of Global Economic Ltd. and acknowledged as one of Canada's leading authorities on economics, says that because we have allowed large numbers of unskilled workers into Canada in recent years, the country's overall productivity has been affected. In the book *The Effects of Mass Immigration on Canadian Living Standards and Society*, Grady writes:

> Growth accounting is a commonly used approach for estimating the impact on productivity of various factors such as education and the age and sex of those who make up the labour force. It involves using earnings weights to distinguish the effects of various factors. When applied over the period from 1990 to 2004, it suggests that immigration has lowered productivity by around 1.5% or 0.15% per year. While this is not very large, it is still significant and runs counter to the claims usually made regarding the productivity-enhancing effect of immigration.

Grady goes on to say:

> Robert Putnam, the Harvard sociologist who made his name studying social capital, has recently been reluctantly forced to come to the conclusion that immigration and diversity are reducing social solidarity and social capital. It is not a long step from this to the conclusion that immigration could undermine productivity. While this type of impact would be very difficult to measure, it could ultimately turn out to be significant.

A rough translation is that there is plenty of evidence to suggest that one of the reasons Canada's productivity is among the lowest in the

G8 (5th), while the US rate is among the highest (2nd), is because of our mass immigration policy. If this is true, then reducing our rate of immigration and limiting admission to those whose skills are required would improve productivity to some degree.

Germany presents an excellent example of how working just a bit harder and longer and delaying retirement a few years can provide a tremendous boost to productivity and thus the economy and standard of living. The average German works about four hours more each week than the average worker in the rest of the European Union. In addition, the average German's retirement age is about three years later than the European average. As a consequence, even during the recent recession the German economy performed well above the European average and, in fact, the latest figures from the European Union indicate that Germany's GDP is about 25 per cent above that of France and the UK.

As you can appreciate, there was tremendous resentment among Germany's working population when they were called upon to essentially bail out a bankrupt Greece. As well as working longer hours than the Greeks, Germans, on average, have to work nine years longer before being eligible for government pensions and, what really drove the Germans crazy, is the fact that about 70 per cent of German residents pay taxes compared to only about 20 per cent in Greece.

The lesson here is: Unless we have a hard-working Germany ready to bail us out, we in Canada had better soon start pulling up our socks. We need to improve our national work ethic or we are going to lose the Canada we know to a few dozen foreign cultures that, in many cases, aren't noted for a national work or tax-paying ethic any better than Greece's.

Another factor that undoubtedly affects productivity in this country is our high rate of taxation. According to the latest figures from Statistics Canada, total tax and non-tax revenue acquired by all levels of government in this country amount to 38.4 per cent of GDP. In the United States, the figure is much lower at 28.2 per cent. In Canada, government spending amounts to 36 per cent of GDP compared to only 31 per cent in the US. It must be noted that these figures are for 2008. Government spending in both countries has obviously skyrocketed since then due to various bailouts and spending incentives to boost flagging economies, but the percentages probably have not changed substantially.

One method of lowering taxes at all three levels of government would be to cut the immigration flow at least in half and insist upon intaking only those for whom good jobs would be immediately available. That act alone would save us untold billions of dollars.

To sum up: It would appear that if we trained our young people better for jobs that actually exist, worked a bit harder and perhaps even a bit longer, reduced immigration to a fraction of what it is today, admitted only the highly skilled, and lowered our taxes, we could probably boost our productivity substantially.

I've got to admit, however, that boosting it by one per cent a year is a mighty tall order. According to Statistics Canada, from 1973 until 1995 productivity growth was only 1.1 per cent a year. During the past decade it has actually dropped to a pitiful 0.7 per cent per year. The US, on the other hand, experienced a rather amazing productivity increase of 2.8 per cent in the first quarter of 2010. This was due almost entirely to union concessions and improved efficiencies thanks to the recession, which forced companies to essentially get more work out of fewer people. Unfortunately, Canada has not learned its lesson as well as the Americans. At least not yet.

In order to achieve the goal suggested by the C.D. Howe report, we would have to pretty well double the rate of productivity growth. In other words, Canadian workers would have to become almost as productive as those in the US.

Can we do it? Of course we can.

Will we?

The answer to that is we'll either have to do it or end up like Greece. Only in our case there won't be any European Union to bail us out. We'll all be in essentially the same boat.

Is Canada's mass immigration policy at least partially to blame for our low productivity?

You can deny it all you want, and many will, but one thing is for darn sure, the huge numbers of unskilled immigrants pouring into our country aren't helping.

And let's be perfectly honest here. A little less socialism in this country might get a few more people working a bit harder.

Hard to believe that we can't increase our productivity by one per cent a year, for goodness' sake. This is the country, after all, that in WWII mobilized ourselves to create the world's third-largest navy and the world's fourth-largest air force in only a couple of years— and in the process pretty well saved Britain's bacon!

It's our bacon that needs saving this time around, so let's get at it. By the way, whatever happened to the 40-hour workweek and why are Ottawa's roads half-empty every Friday morning?

Let's Have More Babies!

The third part of the solution suggested in the C.D. Howe report is to increase the birth rate. Obviously, it's not just in our factories and offices that we've got to work harder. We're not doing a very good job in the bedrooms of the nation either. At least not the kind of work that produces babies!

Canada's fertility rate, like that of many Western nations, continues to fall well below that which is required to maintain a stable population. In other words, a lot more folks are dying than are being born. A fertility rate of 2.1 or 2.2 is what they tell us is needed in order to keep up with those who, as my grandma used to say, "pass over." At last check, Canada's fertility rate was hovering just below 1.5, a fact constantly being used to justify our high rate of immigration.

Most other Western nations have fertility rates that are even lower but rather than increasing immigration in an effort to boost the population and create a younger demographic, many European nations are either slowing rates of immigration drastically or closing the taps entirely.

France, for example, has closed its borders to all but a few immigrants. Holland has rounded up thousands of illegal immigrants and sent them home. Anyone immigrating to the Netherlands today is subjected to an hour-long movie illustrating, among other things, that country's liberal view of homosexuality and sex. Only those who speak Dutch need apply. The June 2010 election in Holland, which gave unprecedented support for far-right-wing parties, very clearly indicated the growing alarm about the manner in which immigrants are failing to integrate into Dutch society.

But it's not just in the Netherlands where concern over immigration is growing. There is widespread pressure from many quarters in Norway, Sweden and Germany to halt all immigration, even though their intake numbers are only a fraction of Canada's.

Many European countries have lower fertility rates than Canada, but not one of them has even considered immigration as a solution to an aging population.

In Sweden, the government has launched a concerted effort to increase productivity and delay the age of retirement. Germany, as previously noted, has already increased its productivity and raised the retirement age to the point where the graying of their population is of little concern. It too has slowed immigration to a trickle.

France is taking steps to combat the unions and get more productivity from its workers and farmers, but what is absolutely astonishing is the manner in which France has been able to increase its fertility rate and drastically curb immigration. France, in addition, sets yearly deportation quotas of between 25,000 and 29,000 as part of its campaign to crack down on illegal immigration.

The French Solution

On several occasions in recent years I have asked listeners of my radio talk show in Ottawa if they believed there was a government policy that would help to convince Canadian families to have more children. In particular, I asked young women if they had more money, would they have more babies.

Many of the callers didn't think there was anything any government could do to boost the country's fertility rate, but towards the end of one of my two-hour programs I did begin to get some calls from younger women who said, in effect, "You know something, Lowell, if there was some way we could get a better tax break; if we just had a bit more money or cheaper child care or something, we would love to have another child or two."

Several young fathers began to say essentially the same thing, enough callers overall to convince me that the high cost of raising children today is at least one of the reasons for our declining fertility rate.